ONCE
UPON
A THERMAL

BOOKS by RICHARD A. WOLTERS

GUN DOG
FAMILY DOG
WATER DOG
INSTANT DOG
BEAU
THE ART AND TECHNIQUE OF SOARING
LIVING ON WHEELS
ONCE UPON A THERMAL

ONCE UPON A THERMAL

BY RICHARD A. WOLTERS

CROWN PUBLISHERS, INC.
NEW YORK

Dedicated . . . to Trux Pratt and his hospitality at the big
square dining room table, the center of Pratt Fall
. . . to all the pilots and their crews whose dinner stories
during contest weeks at Sugarbush helped calm my
nerves and spark this book
. . . to the kind of competitive spirit and camaraderie
found in that room
. . . to our host

Library of Congress Catalog Card Number: 74–80313
Printed in the United States of America
Published simultaneously in Canada by General Publishing Company Limited
Designed by Ruth Smerechniak

Contents

This Book Is About...

ONCE THE CANOPY IS CLOSED YOU'RE PRETTY MUCH COMMIT-
ted to the flight. If you like it, you have said, you might go
on and take your student training. They've put you in the
back seat of the trainer, and although you wouldn't dare say
so, the seat belt and shoulder harness are comforting. Later
you'll chuckle at this first ambivalence, but for now you
might as well go through the motions of these thoughts and
get them out of the way.

The sailplane, so graceful in flight, is clumsy, lopsided,
and out of its element on the ground. Sitting in it, waiting
for takeoff, you feel awkward. You've prepared yourself the
best you can for the new experience, but even now, before
it starts, something seems wrong. The world's already
cockeyed, but you don't realize why until the lowered wing
is lifted off the ground and held level by the wing boy—a
signal to start the flight. Your pilot is at the controls.
Takeoff speed is not as fast as driving your car; some might
giggle or grab on because they're above the ground, flying
—flying parallel to it. When the towplane gathers its speed

and is off, that's when things change. Fast.

Why does the new pilot look down? Is it because he's breaking his earthly ties, for the first time? Is it because he's seeing old familiar things from a new perspective and they're strange and exciting? Weren't trees to be seen from the trunks up? Now, houses seen from the roofs down? Roads seen from all the way around their curves? Cars get smaller and smaller, move slower and slower. Leaves no longer exist; they're blobs of color. So are the fields. Things seem unreal. You're detached. People and their emotions are down there only because you know it.

When you break with below, there is a whole new vista, out and away—mountains, sky, rivers, towns. That spectrum, it's rewarding in the silence.

ONE

The Search

For thousands of years man watched the birds and wanted to fly with them. Stupidly, I spent most of my years watching the girls. But if as a young man I'd known that soaring was the sport of the gods, with a touch of the supernatural, I'd have quit whatever I was at and headed for the nearest gliderport.

Our atmosphere is truly one of our last frontiers; conquering it with powerless wings is a personal achievement for those who love a skill and yearn for challenge and everlasting beauty. Even at my advanced age, I might have missed the whole thing except for an absolute misunderstanding. When soaring was brought to my attention by my friend Phil Gilbert, he was explaining one of the three methods of launching a sailplane into the air. I swear I thought he said, "You'll be flung into the air with a *wench!*"

At my age, I liked the thought of that and so it was that the new frontier engulfed me. But that's all hindsight; what I knew then is where this story begins.

An author between books is like an actor between shows; it's a bad time. For seven years I'd written about dogs—how to train them, hunt with them, live with them, love them, laugh at them . . . and myself. The excitement of field-trialing Tar, my great Labrador retriever, was over. My wife Olive, Tar, and I had traveled from Maine to the Carolinas and coast to coast running the dog circuit at the drop of a pheasant. It took all those years to realize finally that I was sick and tired of being one of the doggy people.

The crowning blow came the day that Tar and I were off by ourselves running in a New Jersey trial. He couldn't put his foot down wrong that day; he finished every series with style and dignity. After the last bird was shot and retrieved, a hard day's work, we took our customary walk while the judges tallied their score sheets. Tar enjoyed our little ritual as much as I did. I always made it a point to tell him how magnificent he was and how much I loved him. It would be ridiculous even to suggest that he understood my language, but after eight hours of being a stern master and he being an obedient servant we had to take this time to get things back to normal. After all, he wasn't going home to live in a kennel, he was going home to take his place as a member of the family. The competition was over; he loved it and so did I, and this was our way to clear the air of the master and servant roles and become two animals that enjoyed each other.

In spite of all his ribbons, there are many dogs better than Tar. But not that day! I couldn't wait to get him off alone. As soon as we hit the woods I gave him a friendly cuff, the signal to start our game. He'd dart and weave in circles around me, growl and bark and jam to a halt, stand erect; I swear he'd start to laugh at me. He'd let me grab him, then over and over we'd roll. That's the kind of love a working dog likes. After he'd dragged me through the dirt by the sleeve, I'd settle him down and we'd talk. He wouldn't seem to pay much attention and sometimes even go to sleep when I was in the middle of my love speech. But just as the roughhousing took the tension of the day out of him, my little speech made me feel better.

That day was different. While I was being dragged along the ground our ceremony was interrupted by Mrs. Anne Roosevelt. She had sought out Tar to tell him, too, like me, what a grand competitor he was and that she had never seen a dog that loved his work so much. She gave him a hug and congratulated him on what she was sure would be first place.

But Tar didn't get his first place that day . . . nor even a fourth. Other competitors wanted me to file a complaint, but that wasn't our style. I had done battle with both judges over kennel club business in the past and everybody at the trial knew it. I won that battle some years ago and this was their revenge. They couldn't beat me so they were going to beat my dog.

Another Roosevelt came to mind as Tar and I drove home empty-handed. He was a President and had had a dog named Fala. I'd only been a boy at the time but remembered the newspaper stories about the savage attacks on FDR's private life. They spread rumors against his wife, children, and even Fala. That was their mistake. During the political campaign that ensued, the President chided his opponents not for their attack on his wife and children but for the snide remarks about his dog. He won reelection by a landslide. I asked Tar as we drove home if the pretty lady, FDR's daughter-in-law, sensed that this attack was going to happen and that's why she'd come over to give him the pat. Tar didn't seem to care; he rolled over and went back to sleep, half on and half off the front seat.

It was childish at forty-eight to react to that episode and make it into a big deal, but now I wanted out of the sport. I'd had it up to my neck with the dog people. Over the years Tar had proved what he could do, so I felt we were both ready to retire from that scene.

That was my last field trial and in a matter of weeks my term was up as president of our field trial club. Unlike FDR I didn't want to be reelected.

But it's not that easy to walk away from something that has been an important part of your life. My five books on dogs were as much as I felt I wanted to say at the time but I didn't want to stop writing. I must have been some bad news to live with during that period, and I realized it when a good friend stopped over to the house one night and tried as hard as he could to get me to play golf with him. Even my wife wanted me to try it. I refused. Chasing a ball around on the grass to drop it into a cup wasn't my cup of tea.

Secretly, at first, I started a search for a new thing but I didn't have the slightest idea what it was going to be. Tennis was out. I'd spent fifteen years at that game. I already had a cabinetful of skeet trophies. Thinking of owning a sailboat again made me shudder; it was too much work each spring and besides I was looking for something new to learn. I had enough big-game trophies on my walls and I'd traveled halfway around the world collecting all the fishing lies needed for a full lifetime and writing about fishing was a bore. The last thing I wrote on that subject was for one of the men's magazines and all the editor wanted was stories about how I almost died in eight inches of water fighting a trout that was bigger than my grandmother.

If a man wants to drive himself crazy I know now how to proceed: search for something and not know what it is he's seeking. Tar at least was enjoying his retirement.

One day I sat down and started to put my problem down on paper, thinking that might help my search. I only found out things about myself that I didn't like; it brought me no closer to a new project unless the new thing was a depression. I'd always been a bad sleeper, but now my sleep was much worse. For years my sleepless nights were the best part of the day. I'd lie in bed working out problems, memorizing the angles of the skeet field, or how to take a fish I knew was in a certain pool, or how to handle the starting line of a boat race when the wind was quartering off the starboard, or how to make a certain joint in a cabinet I was building, or a new way to train my setters to point game; or I'd memorize ballads to sing with the ten guitar chords I knew, or how to write about those things. Now I was lying awake trying to think about something to *think* about.

One friend suggested that maybe I should take up making money and I said no, I didn't want a failure on my record. Another suggested sex but after thinking about that in bed I decided age was against me, and besides, in those years it wasn't something an upstanding citizen could write about. What a mistake. If I'd have taken up sex I could have been in on the ground floor of that exploding porno business. Although I'm still not an expert on that subject, I really believe the material of this book is even more exciting and the competition is just as keen. When I think about it, soaring and sex have a lot in common—they're both a sensational experience and with both you don't know where you're going to land. But I still insist if a man's going to write a book he should write it about something he understands, hence this book is about soaring. That was the affair I was going to have later, but falling in love was still a year away. In the meantime I did find a girl friend to occupy my time.

One day in the midst of my search for my new thing, I was walking down a Manhattan street and passed a foreign car showroom. Like a high school boy, I fell in love at first sight with the car in the window. She was a hot little racer and I had to have her, but it proved to be puppy love and the affair didn't last. I bought her and prepared her for racing. Many a weekend we spent at racing school where we got to know each other very well. It really wasn't her fault that we didn't make it together; she did the best she could but I guess I lost my nerve. It began and ended one day at the Lime Rock racetrack. Like all beginners I didn't understand the strategy. I was pushing her for all she was worth but she responded in elegant fashion. She quickly taught me that a light touch was all she needed. By the middle of the race we were in love; during the last lap it was all over. As we were preparing to overtake a beautiful green Morgan I sensed that it was going out of control and took an evasive action by moving to the outside of the turn. With a sickening noise the Morgan spun and hurtled over the bank. When the race was over I drove the circuit to the scene of the crash. A young boy, half my age, was sitting crying next to his demolished racing green Morgan. The roll bar saved his life and his belts kept him from even being scratched. I sat and talked to him. He wasn't upset because of shock; he was upset because he didn't know how to tell his father that he wanted another green Morgan. That ended my affair. I never raced again. I didn't have a father who could buy me another mistress if I destroyed the one I had worked hard to buy. Like Tar, she too was retired and I went on to search further.

I hated to think that I'd given up that sport before I conquered it, and I still believe that it wasn't a loss of nerve but something else that I'd come to learn. We Americans seem to be brought up to believe that we can all be President. There is a part of our sports scene that we just don't learn. All we want to do is win. To play a game the best you can and enjoy it is not for us. Sportsmanship is something the Europeans know about, and they do perform their sports with style. We bring too much aggression to our sports, and this became quite evident to me with the car racing buffs. They were a humorless bunch, and they all had their secrets that would make them win. They lacked a compassion and warmth for their fellow sportsmen, and at forty-eight I wasn't about to start that game. Seeing the crash was my excuse to get out.

That last race was on a Sunday. That night I felt as low

as a flat tire and seriously considered taking up drinking
. . . a good book still has to be written on that sport. I sat
at the typewriter and mapped out an outline. It looked
rather good and I got excited. This idea would solve all my
problems but when I tried the idea on my wife she laughed
at me and said, "With your ability with a bottle you couldn't
get through the first chapter." I went to bed.

The beautiful thing about any search, especially if you
don't know what you're looking for, is that you never know
where or when you might find what you want. Of course,
you can only be that philosophical after the fact. In the
meantime Monday morning slowly arrived after another
restless night of having nothing to be restless about. I must
have shaved, dressed, and had breakfast because I was getting on my commuter train when Phil Gilbert sidled up to
me and said, "Don't tell me, let me guess. Your house
burned down?"

I shook my head.

"You're being sued?"

"Nope."

"The IRS has caught up with you?"

"Look, Phil," I started at him with a false testy tone, "you
lawyer types think that problems only revolve around
money and possessions. Other people's problems are your
bank account."

"If all my clients paid me as much as you do I'd have to
turn to writing to make an easy living and I wouldn't have
to look far for a crazy character to write about."

I feigned being stabbed in the heart and we both
laughed.

Phil, a grand guy, one of those Park Avenue lawyers with
his name listed at the top on the door, is a very perceptive
fellow. He's the only New York lawyer I've ever known who
has more jokes than Harvard has lawbooks. Laughing at his
punch lines has been an easy way for me to get what is
considered the best legal advice in the country—all free

good tips on the market that I didn't have the nerve to take.

We took our usual place in the smoking car and lit up. "Look, I've got something for you that's going to make you feel better."

"Well, it better not be one of your jokes." I tried to discourage him by opening my *New York Times.*

"What did you do, crack up your car?"

"No, but I quit racing."

"Well, pal"—one of Phil's favorite expressions when he's about to open up on a guy—"I've been telling you all along that you're too old and wouldn't have the reflexes. Now, pal, I've got just the thing for you."

"Sorry, I've thought of it and discarded it. Look, Phil, you don't understand. You lawyers know about golf and bridge and the only competitive thing you do is have foot-races with ambulances."

He opened his newspaper to signal that the conversation was over, but he wasn't reading it. We've played this game so often. Finally, I said, "OK, Phil, what's your idea?"

"Look, pal"—here he goes again—"I've given you more million-dollar ideas . . ."

"Phil," I interrupted, "forget the million-dollar ideas and just give me the million dollars."

"This time I'm going to collect my fee. I've solved your problem! I just spent three fantastic days at Sugarbush, Vermont, and started taking soaring lessons."

"*Sewing* lessons?" I screwed up my face in disbelief.

"No, soaring!" And with that he flung his arms outstretched as if they were wings, flapped like a bird, and almost knocked the pipe out of my mouth.

That simple conversation was five years and $20,000 ago.

By the time we arrived at Grand Central, Phil had me enthusiastic; just the thought of gliding or soaring or whatever they wanted to call it seemed glamorous and exciting. I rushed off the train and ran over to Abercrombie and Fitch and asked Mr. Smith in the book department for anything he had on gliding. He told me that he'd had some other requests lately and knew that there was no book written in the U.S. on the subject. At first I was disappointed because I wanted some background in the subject besides Phil's meager but glowing descriptions of his ten flights in three days. Then it dawned on me, if there was no such book, I'd write it.

My search ended that instant. I asked the manager if I could borrow his phone. He sent me back to his office and I called Frank Taylor, my swinging friend who was the editorial director of one of the biggest publishing houses in New York.

"Frank, you said you wanted my next book. You've got it! Nothing's been written on the subject in this country and I'm going to do the classic. It's on soaring. I'll call it *The Art and Technique of Soaring.*"

"No, Frank. *Soaring,* not sewing." I put down the phone and put my arms out to the side and flapped.

Two lucky things happened. One I had guessed and one I didn't know. The thing I guessed was that Frank would jump at the idea because he was the most imaginative book publisher in the city, and the thing I didn't know was that he was going off that morning to Europe.

"Great idea," was his response. "We'll have lunch on it in a month." His parting words were, "If we can sell as many gliding books as you've sold dog books, we'll have America barking all over the sky."

I was saved from my own enthusiasm. I had a month's reprieve, time at least to learn the gliding language.

That night in my study I had some second thoughts about my ridiculous decision. I'd committed myself but that's the way I'd always worked. I wasn't a young kid. Quite to the contrary, at my age with two children in school, a wife and kingdom in suburbia that required a minister of the treasury to keep the house out of the hands of the tax collector, I was going to go fly. Motorless! I had a restless night.

At three in the morning I got up, turned on the tape

recorder next to the bed and dictated this input: "Ask your-self in the morning, after the first coffee, 'Why the hell do I want to fly?' Check insurance policy. Go to roof in office, look down, and see what happens. Reconsider all this in the light of day and decide if I might be losing my rivets."

After a fine purposeful, restless night of making sure I didn't fall out of bed without a chute on, I decided to broach the subject at breakfast. "Dear," I said, waiting for her to put her cup down in the saucer, "I think I'll take up soaring . . ."

After a pause, she said, "You already started . . . in bed last night."

"I didn't say *snoring*. I said soaring. You know, gliding." I flapped my arms.

"I heard you. Now you're going to fly."

"Is that all you have to say? I could get killed, or something."

"I'm not worried. You knew when to stop racing cars, and besides, soaring is safer."

"How do you know so much?"

"Phil told me."

TWO

In the Beginning

IT WAS EASY FOR AN OLD REPORTER TO FIND OUT WHERE ONE could learn to glide without going all the way to Vermont. The third phone call led me to one Arthur Hurst at a Wall Street phone number.

"Mr. Hurst, I'm interested in gliding or sailplaning and was told that . . ."

"That's good," he interrupted. "We call it soaring."

OK, I thought, at least now I've learned the name of the sport. Art was extremely helpful and seemed to know what questions I wanted to ask. When it came to how safe the sport was he said, "Drive up to Wurtsboro Airport in the Catskill Mountains on Saturday and I'll give you a ride, but be careful driving—it's more dangerous than the flight we'll take."

Wurtsboro Airport didn't exactly have an International Arrival Building like all the airports I'd visited. In fact, when I arrived it didn't have a john that was working. Now I knew why Art laughed when I asked him if we should meet at the bar; that turned out to be a guy selling hamburgers in a shack. All that has improved by now. The shack has been torn down. The food has improved, too . . . you bring your own. As for the school of aviation that Art mentioned, that turned out to be an office where you paid your bill.

I had tried to figure out what Art was going to look like; after all, you want to have some idea about the person you are going to trust with your life. He turned out to be good looking, in fact better than good looking, typical of what you would expect to work on Wall Street. His handshake and smile exuded confidence, but it was the place that shook me. I had expected much more and was starting to lose my nerve. He noticed my shifting from foot to foot and told me there was an outhouse behind the hangar.

Halfway to the outhouse I worked out my plan. I could sneak around behind the hangar and run for the car, drive off, and no one would be the wiser. How had I ever gotten myself trapped into this situation? Then I thought of Frank Taylor and the book I had promised.

As Art and I walked around the field, he did his best to explain everything there was to see; but I wasn't paying full attention. My thoughts were having a great big fight with me. When he suggested a hamburger and coffee at the shack, I bought a pack of cigarettes to calm my nerves but was afraid to light up for fear my shaking hands would give me away. I met another soaring pilot named Gordie Lamb. There was some friendly chatter about my wanting to fly to see if I liked soaring. I noticed that I was doing a lot of high-pitched laughing and stopped to ask myself, "What the hell is so funny?"

This fellow Lamb was very friendly. He had spent years as a navy pilot, and even I knew that that was one of the best pilot trainings in the world. I had trouble learning to ride a bicycle. What was I ever thinking about when I let Phil talk me into trying this nonsense? I questioned Gordie about all the planes he had flown, and he rattled off sets of numbers that sounded to me like the quantum theory.

It dawned on me that I should ask Art his experience. After all, getting information by phone for a story was one thing. If the information was wrong the paper could print a retraction. Wrong information in this game is an obituary. When Art explained that he had had his license three weeks, I excused myself and headed for the back of the hangar.

The next thing I remember, someone was strapping me into the cockpit. In my hometown is a place called Sing Sing where a chair and straps mean only one thing. I felt at home. The guy who was stuffing me in and pulling on the straps was wearing what appeared to me to be a suspicious ear-to-ear grin. I could see no good reason at this time for that smile. When he had me firmly packed down he patted my knee and said, "You'll be all right." He closed the canopy, locked it, gave me that knowing grin, and ran.

I sat staring into the back of Art's head and my brain started to race. Art had one clump of hair that stood straight up. I remembered as a boy having the same problem and my Mother combing it so hard that she cut my scalp; then I remembered her telling me not to climb the tree, so I did, got dizzy, and fell out and broke my arm; then I remem . . . God, was my whole life going to pass before me like a drowning man's last seconds?

I pulled myself together as the pedals started to move at my feet and the stick waggled between my legs. I heard Art say something like, "Are you ready?" I didn't bother to answer. The towplane parked in front of us came to life and so did I.

Before I knew it we were airborne, drifting a few feet off the ground. Then we headed skyward as the towplane lifted off. To my great surprise there was absolutely no sensation. I could make no sense out of what the dual control pedals and the stick were doing pumping around in my part of the cockpit, but Art seemed to know; he kept our sailplane on the end of the towrope as if it were glued to one spot behind the airplane. As the plane turned and climbed, we were riveted behind it. The towplane circled and climbed over the airport. As I looked down, things didn't seem real. Although I'd seen this view hundreds of times from the little windows on commercial flights, now it was panoramic.

Art asked, "How you doing?"

"Oh, great!"

"We're at two thousand and we'll release at three thousand."

That brought me back to life inside the canopy. I struggled with my harness so I could lean to the side and see past Art's head to look at the instrument panel. I watched as the hand on the dial neared three thousand. Then Art reached for a knob and said, "Here we go."

I thought I knew what he meant, but at that instant a shot was fired. The adrenalin surged. My eyes darted to the wing tips to see if they were still on. We turned and dove to the right . . . dove for the earth.

In an instant we were back in level flight. I must have reacted or said something.

"Sorry I forgot to warn you about the loud noise of the release. Scared hell out of me the first time I heard it. That turn we just made," Art continued in a calm voice, "was the release maneuver to clear the rope."

His calm voice reassured me and things inside me got back to normal.

We were now in free flight and the thought of it was a marvel. The whispering of the air while flying was a new phenomenon. It dawned on me that I hated lawn mowers, outboard motors, even electric motors; no wonder car racing wasn't for me. I realized all this at three thousand feet —in a whole new world.

I was about to tell Art how exciting it all was when he said, "Can you see this needle? We're going to go up."

"We're climbing on a thermal, an invisible column of warm air," Art started to say in a tone of voice Wall Streeters use to explain stocks to little old ladies. "The sun is actually powering our flight. The ground is heated at different rates according to its makeup. A pile of rocks will heat up faster than a marsh, or a cliff facing the sun will be warmer than one in the shade. Understand?"

"Well, I think so," I replied.

"You know that the sun doesn't heat the air; it heats the ground and in turn the ground heats the air above it. The hotter the ground, the hotter the air. Got it?"

"Ya, I guess so."

"Let me explain it this way. See that plowed field below? Over there. See it?" He pointed. "That dark soil of the field will absorb more heat than the grove of trees next to it. The air over the field will become warmer than the air over the trees. Hot air rises and it's all that simple. The hotter air will eventually get so warm that it'll bust away from the surrounding air and up she'll go. The air over the trees will rush in to replace the air that went up. In turn it'll be warmed from the ground and up it'll go. That's a thermal."

"It's like a bubble in a pot of water that starts to boil?" I asked.

"Well, yes, you can think of it that way. I'd say it's more like a column. We fly into that bubble, as you say, and by circling tightly in it we stay in the updraft. Up goes the air and carries us with it. That's lift, and it can be as strong as a thousand feet a minute or more. That means it can take us up at that rate. Thermals of three hundred to five hundred feet per minute are average around here. But also, if hot air rises, cool air sinks. Between thermals you will find cool air, or sink. Sink can be just as strong or weak as thermals."

"How can you tell where the thermals are when you're flying?" I asked.

"You'll learn to read the terrain and make rather good guesses as to where thermals will kick off. Then the column of lift will drift on the wind as it goes up, so on the downwind side of a plowed field or a group of buildings, or whatever it is that's making the thermal, is the place to search for the updraft."

"How can you tell when you're near it or in its center?"

"This instrument does it for you. It's a variometer or vario. Some have noisemakers that will start to beep when you're in lift. The louder the beep, the stronger the lift. We're getting close to it. Watch this needle start to go up. Here we go!"

I stretched to the right to see past his head where his hand was pointing and with that he banked sharply to the left, throwing me gently against my straps. We stayed in the tight turn and circled. Around and around we churned, and I giggled with delight as we climbed up to the fleecy white wisps of cloud on invisible power.

Three times we found the thermal lift and three times, to my amusement, we climbed. Then we found no more and slowly sank back toward the automobiles, people, houses. I sensed that the flight would soon be over and tried to drink in the view and commit it to memory. Art said something about a pattern and started the landing maneuver. Four months of flying and he was a master. The landing was exciting; the trees moved up to join us. I didn't feel or remember the touchdown. And then we were still.

I don't know how long I sat there trying to get used to the idea of the firm ground; it was unreal.

Gordie Lamb and some other fellows came out to help us pull the ship off the runway. I remember very little about the rest of that day. I did go to the school of aviation—that is, the office—sign some papers and give them a check for my training that was to start the next day. I know I had thousands of questions, and I know I asked them, but I don't remember the questions or the answers. I do remember how impressed I was with all the time the guys gave me. As I look back I think I know why the rest of that day faded from memory. I was so relaxed and relieved that my long search was over that I wanted to wallow in that pleasure. The real work was going to start the next day.

It wasn't until months later that I came to understand another part of that day that I liked. It was the people in this sport. They all take a keen interest in the newcomer. If the newcomer is not a wise guy and a know-it-all, they'll go all out to bring him along. We didn't have a formal club but the fraternal spirit was there. We would be flying together, ground-handling the planes for one another, swapping tools and information. This was so different from dog-trialing and the car racing. This was the kind of people I used to hunt and fish with; there was a camaraderie and I liked it.

Although soaring is safe, anytime you fly there is a certain element of danger. But that's true about car racing, too. I came to note that the soaring pilot had a compassion even for his competitor. In only a few years after that first day when Art Hurst and Gordie Lamb were so kind to me, I'd be in direct competition with them in the U.S. Nationals. They never stopped helping me until the one day I finally beat them both in a regional competition. Then they razzed me and told me how ungrateful I was for all their help. These two and many more like them were a special part of what I was going to love about soaring.

THREE

The School of Aviation

THE FLIGHT WAS SO SATISFYING THAT SLEEPING WAS NO trouble that night. Besides, I didn't have enough knowledge to know what my problems were going to be.

But that soon changed. At nine sharp the next morning I was at the airport. The place looked deserted. A few training ships were down on the line, and the only soul around was one of the line boys standing near the trainer, which I figured he had just brought out of the hangar. I meandered down to talk to him.

"Where is everybody?" I asked as I came up to him.

"Who are you looking for?"

"I have an appointment with an instructor."

"Oh, what's your name?"

"Wolters."

"Good! I'm George, your instructor."

I know my lips must have formed the word *no* and my eyes had to give away my thoughts. George wasn't even shaving more than once a week. I had a son older than that, God, in my office, kids that age couldn't be trusted to run a Xerox machine these days.

George caught it all and laughed. "Don't worry. I've had a lot of experience. My dad owns the airport."

That didn't cut any ice with me. I knew a kid whose father owned a bank and he traded on the fact and went to jail. Reluctantly, I began my training.

Of course I knew that I'd have no trouble learning to fly a sailplane. I'd always been a good athlete and caught on to new things quickly. The first time on skis and after only twenty minutes on the beginners' slope the instructor said, "Come on, let's go to the top of the intermediate trail, you'll do fine." And I did. After about the third or fourth flight, George was still showing extreme patience. I had the controls and he said, "Give me a steep turn to the right."

I thought a moment then went to work.

"No. No! To the right."

"Oh, excuse me."

Then I went to work again. I'm not too sure what did happen to the plane but George, who was sitting at the dual controls behind me, sucked in his breath. There was a pause, then he said slowly, "What in the name of God would you call that maneuver?"

Embarrassed at my inept proclivities I quipped back, "That was a practice dive-bomb run," and I chuckled to try to clear the air.

"Mr. Wolters"—and I caught that Mr.—"soaring is not a funny sport. If you want to kill yourself with laughter, don't take me with you."

The maneuver actually established the student-instructor roles. I was scared to death that I'd pull another blooper. At first, I had visions of getting into the sailplane and taking command of the controls and flying it away into the heavens. My dream was shattered.

On our next flight he said, "As soon as I get her off the ground I want you to take over and fly us on tow. The position you want to keep, on the end of the towline, is directly behind the towplane. Keep the top of the towplane's vertical stabilizer lined up with the tow pilot's head. Understand?"

"Yes, yes. But what's the vertical stabilizer?"

George took a deep breath, explained it to me, and said, "Do you know what the pilot's head looks like?"

Dejectedly I answered something like "Well, I'm starting to think a pilot's head doesn't look anything like mine."

He laughed a one-syllable laugh and answered, "Come on, Dick, you're doing just fine."

I figured that that was right out of his instructor's manual, under the heading, "Give the Student Confidence." It did and things were back to a starting position until I took over the controls on tow.

I remembered how easy it was for Art to keep the ship glued to the spot in space as though riveted onto the towplane's tail. I was determined! The instant we drifted to the right I slammed all controls left! This wasn't going to get away from *me*. Surprised, we passed the towplane on the left and I pushed everything to the right. I was horrified. Off we swung to the right and I could hear in my mind's ear Captain Bligh's command, "Hard aport! Mr. Christian," and I did. Oh, how the mind plays dirty tricks on us. At that instant I remembered as a boy being on the stage of the local movie theatre. Between shows, I'd entered a Yo-Yo contest and lost in the finals. I was reentered and winning that contest today. I had a bag of tricks on the end of that string that would have brought down the house.

George wasn't impressed.

"Mr. Wolters"—we were back to *that*—"you're not driving a bulldozer."

As he brought us in for a landing to end that day's lessons, I started to wonder how he was going to handle things. Would he want to give me my money back? Would he do it by letter? Would his dad offer me extra money to give up and try another sport?

When we got out of the ship I watched his every expression to try to fathom what he was thinking. I'd be damned if I'd ask because I really knew how I was doing. I got nothing from his face, but was relieved when he said, "See you next Saturday."

The intervening week was good and bad. I'll give you the bad news first.

I was inundated, distraught, angry, and disappointed. Wasn't I the guy who shot a twenty-two out of twenty-five at my first round of skeet? Had I lost my touch? Was I too old for car racing and too old for soaring? It was the book that had me depressed. Thank goodness, I never breathed a word of it to any of the guys at the airport. Twenty-two-year-old George would split his breeches laughing if he heard that one. The pilots would have smiled politely to each other. I might have had precision timing with a fly rod in a stream and good footwork on a tennis court, but I was sure a clod in a cockpit. By Wednesday night I'd beaten myself down so far that I started to work out the details in bed, on how I was going to break the news to Frank Taylor when he came back in two weeks from Europe. "Oh, Frank, I looked into it further and found that it would be a lot of work and that the market was so small that we couldn't sell enough books." Hell, that wasn't any good; he'd told me it was a coming sport and it'd be good to get in on the ground floor. "Frank, my doctor says that . . ." Nuts, that's not going to work. "Bad news, Frank. I can't hack it. I can't do the book. I can't seem to get the hang of it. I can't even remember my instructor's name, let alone what he says to me from one lesson to the next . . ."

That was the breakthrough. That was the good news! I couldn't seem to remember what George was saying to me. It was so obvious. While I was flying and trying to do what he asked for, he'd start to talk about it even after I'd finished the maneuver. I'd be into my next problem and he'd still be talking about my last one. I'd just turn him off, since I'd survived the past antics and the present shenanigans could still kill me. The answer to all this was a tape recorder.

Thursday night I bought a small cassette tape.

Friday night I built a sensational Rube Goldberg accessory for the tape out of some leather straps, some buckles from my kid's knapsack, and a piece of one of my wife's old girdles.

Saturday morning, with confidence, I walked out to join George at the flight line all dressed in my new rig. As I got close, George forgot his usual greeting. He gawked in amazement at the contraption.

I walked closer. He frowned.

I'd made a very comfortable brassierelike affair to hold the tape recorder firmly against my chest.

"What do you think we're doing. Going to the moon?"

"George, I just want to tape your golden voice to capture all the complimentary remarks you make about my natural flying ability."

"Holy cow! I'm going to be on the air."

With that we climbed in and strapped up.

"I'm attaching the microphone to my shoulder strap so it'll record your voice."

"No," suggested George, "I'll hold it in my hand. It's more professional."

"Ladies and gentlemen," he started seriously in a deep rich tone, "this is George Barone, your station D.O.D. newscaster reporting live from the back of a two-twenty-two sailplane. We are about to witness a major setback to the advancement of aviation. The noted author and sportsman, Richard Wolters, is about to take a motorless airplane off the ground and fly it around in the sky. This is a feat any fourteen-year-old can perform with ease.

"Ladies and gentlemen, the launching airplane is about to be attached to the motorless plane. The scene is a tense one. The spectators are being herded back to a safe distance and the area is being cleared. Mr. Wolters seems a little nervous and is resetting his flying goggles and reading specs that sit on the end of his nose. This is it! From my vantage point, with all insurance paid up, we will be witnessing this spectacular event. Now I see the pilot is reaching for the controls. He has his hand on the stick. No, he has taken his hand off the stick and is fixing his brassiere full of electronic gear.

"There is the signal! There is the signal! The pilot has extended his thumb up. He looks past his white flying scarf toward the wing boy. The wing boy gets the signal, all is A-OK. The wing is being lifted! Mr. Wolters is pushing the stick forward for the takeoff trim. The stick is being pushed forward for the takeoff. If I sound breathless while witnessing this event, it's because Mr. Wolters is supposed to be moving the stick forward for the takeoff position and he seems to have forgotten. Hey, stick forward! Good, now we can go."

"George!" I finally yelled. "Shut up. I can't think. Thank goodness I didn't bring a movie camera to record my training, or you'd be sitting in the back seat putting on your makeup."

"We're moving! We're moving, ladies and gentlemen," George said excitedly. "The plane is going down the runway. If Mr. Wolters will get the stick out of that forward start position and ease it back, we might get airborne. Repeat, ladies and gentlemen, if he'll bring the stick back we'll get airborne. Stick back! Good. That's it, now we'll take a moment out for a commercial from your friendly undertaker. Stay tuned. We'll be back in sixty seconds. I hope."

Goodness only knows if the tape recorder really helped me learn to fly, but it was great therapy between the weekend lessons. I played those tapes day and night. I relived each lesson. At least, with my butt safely affixed to something on the ground, I could recall each flight and study what George was really saying. If he used the phrase "coordinate your turn" once, he used it a thousand times. I started to practice it every free moment I had. It's like that kid's game where you rub your stomach with one hand and pat the top of your head with the other. It's right hand, right foot; left hand, left foot; right foot, right hand; left foot, left hand. It takes real concentration, especially on a noisy subway, in a busy office, or at a business lunch. Did you ever see someone who talks to himself walking down the street? The pedestrians give him plenty of sidewalk room. The same thing happens learning to coordinate your turn as you zigzag down the street . . . right foot, right hand . . . left foot, left hand. My wife threatened to sleep in the guest room if I didn't get the hang of the coordinated turn. Fast.

All of our flights had been twenty-minute up-and-down affairs. We'd take off, do some turns and some stalls. By tightening the tape recorder straps around my chest, I learned how to keep the stomach in its proper place during spins. We'd practice flying level, then after a few more turns we'd have to go in for a landing.

Then one day that changed. A good stiff northwest wind was blowing against the thousand-foot ridge that paralleled the airport. What a day! What a flight! George explained that the wind blowing against the ridge would be diverted upward and we could fly on a wave of air as it lifted to get over the ridge. He called it ridge lift. We had to stay on the windward side, and with his hands he showed me why. On the lee side the wind would go down and you'd go down with it. All pilots use their hands to describe flight. I was so pleased. It was the first time I'd understood the hand language. After doing the usual lesson at altitude, instead of preparing to land at one thousand feet we moved in toward the ridge. At times our wing was only yards from the trees. It was so exciting. When George explained that the ridge went for a hundred miles, all the way down into Pennsylvania and we could ride the ridge lift the whole way, the very thought of it was mind boggling. We stayed up for more than an hour, flying the ridge. The view was breath-taking. Then George almost ruined the whole thing. "Which way is the airport?" he sprang at me.

I was never one to have a good sense of direction. The first day in college I left the class to find the men's room and missed the whole first lecture while I tried to retrace my steps. When George asked that question, I did some fast thinking. Looking ahead I couldn't see the airport, so I stabbed at the answer. "It's behind us."

"Good," said George, so I straightened my white flying scarf with a flourish.

That day gave me a desire to do more than write a book. I now wanted to be a pilot. I wanted to be able to take off, fly to that ridge, and be in command of the plane, the wind, and the ridge below. That was my goal. That's all I wanted.

It's hard to remember exactly when I started to feel comfortable in the new environment, but about the eighteenth flight I was getting the hang of the language, both verbal and hand variety. George was saying less and less into the tape and I might have been getting a little cocky. The day he started muttering something about getting me ready for a solo flight, Frank Taylor arrived back from Europe. I strutted to the promised luncheon appointment at Sardi's restaurant. My hands were nimbly dancing over the famous cold salmon blue plate as I went all out to impress Frank with my newfound skill as a flier. The high point of the lunch was when I was in the middle of a hand demonstration of an incipient spin. An author friend of Frank's stopped by our table, I was introduced, and Frank's tag line was "He's one of our aviation authors." I didn't act smug, but I did have a problem taking my hand out of the incipient spin to shake hands. On first try I missed. I made a fast recovery and on the second pass I had it made and gave Frank's friend a warm shake.

That lunch was both a success and a failure. It was a success because Frank paid for it on his expense account, we settled on a good contract for the training book, my ego was pleased with the sound of the words "aviation author," and Frank reminded me that my flying was now tax deductible. I glided back to the office. It was a failure because when I took my next flying lesson it must have made me consider myself George's equal. Nothing went right. *Nothing* went right! When I finally landed, George burned up my recorder tape with nonflying language, and I didn't need the usual hand demonstration to understand what he was saying.

That was the end of the *thought,* let alone the talk, of my solo flight. What could I have been thinking about on that landing? Like a porpoise I was in and out of the air. Even the takeoff was sloppy and the tow must have looked like I was drunk. When George kicked the plane into a spin and told me to recover it, all I could do was haul back on the stick like I was trying to pull it back up into the sky with a lever. That only put us into a tighter spin, so I pulled up harder. I felt relieved when George sneered into the microphone, "We'll take a station break while I've got the stick." He went through the spin recovery procedure with ease, and while I was wiping the perspiration off my face he continued talking into the tape, "Ladies and gentlemen, that maneuver was not in the scheduled program and since your announcer has a hot date tonight that he expects to keep, your ace reporter had to step in to keep from going off the air permanently. And now we'll turn you back to our pilot. It's all yours again, Mr. Wolters."

Needless to say, I felt swamped, and to follow that with a landing that bounced George's behind all over the airport, I once again had the desire to disappear. At the snack bar, Gordie Lamb laughed and tried to tell me that any landing in which you walk away, and do no damage, is a good one. He also said that it could have been better. I was embarrassed that anyone had seen it. But Gordie told me something I've always remembered. "We've all had flights like that in our training. Every instructor expects it. George was rough on you because he wants you to remember it. It's part of the learning curve. But," and Gordie hesitated. I had the feeling that he was doing it for emphasis. "But," he continued, "when you make a goof flying you must recognize it and snap yourself together. You've just learned that one mistake leads to a second and a third. That, on the ground, is known as a bad day. In the air we don't have bad days. When you catch a first error, correct for it and use your head and be ready to see that the second one doesn't happen. Look, you're going to be a good pilot, even George says so. Come on, I'll buy you a Coke."

That was the first indication I'd had of George's real opinion. I did a lot of thinking about what Gordie said and after the next few flights even I had the feeling that I was starting to *think* and not just do things mechanically. Now the solo flight was something I wanted to do for its own sake. I could taste it. As much as I wanted to do it I refused to ask George. I knew he was holding me off, wanting me to explode with the desire—and I damn near did. I caught myself following him around the airport like a puppy dog, hoping he'd say something that would lead me closer to that solo.

After each flight I expected George to say, "OK, now I want you to solo." Then I expected long verbal instructions on what to expect. I knew what he was going to say. In my mind's ear I'd heard it a dozen times, and I even had the answers ready for the questions I knew he'd ask. But it never came. Each time we'd land and get out of the ship, I'd throw a glance at him because I had even figured out the expression he'd have before he made the historic pronouncement. But it didn't come. It really never did.

The nearest he came to it was one evening after a few flight lessons. He walked toward the hangar and said, "I'm going to start getting these ships into the hangar. Why don't you take a flight."

I was in the middle of saying, "I'll give you a hand moving the . . ." when I realized what he had said. I stopped dead in my tracks and just watched him walk away. As he disappeared I kept thinking, "That's not the way it's supposed to happen. No one will even have the champagne ready." Hadn't I worked it all out in bed? I hadn't told my old father about my training and I was going to call him long distance and say, "Dad, I'm going to solo in a sailplane today." I even worked out the tone of voice to use so he wouldn't be frightened.

Hadn't I worked out how I'd sit in the cockpit just before takeoff so the gallery would feel confident about my big step? I visualized reassuring my wife. I'd be very business-like in the cockpit and give the wing boy loud and clear directions. Nothing was working out as I'd planned! I turned toward the trainer and glanced around the airport. Everyone had gone home. I was alone and as I climbed in I thought to myself, Mac Roman is not even here to perform the shirttail cutting ceremony that was traditional for all student pilots. Then I remember thinking I shouldn't be so disappointed that there was nobody around to congratulate me if I made it . . . the same friends would be absent if I didn't.

FOUR

The New World

CHRISTMAS NIGHT I WAS SITTING LOOKING AT ALL THE GOOD-ies I'd collected that day. I had a new wallet to house my two-month-old student's pilot license, a pair of warm flying boots, two—not one but two—white silk flying scarves, a flight calculator that I didn't understand, a book called *Flight*, and two neckties. One tie had all kinds of early aircraft and balloons all over it, the other had dogs. Someone in the family hadn't gotten the word. Graciously I'd given my wife a full year's subscription to *Soaring* magazine. I knew she'd enjoy that—and she did. About eight that holiday night, when still not a creature was stirring, she looked up from the magazine and said, "I see in an ad here that there's a KA–8 for sale and the price looks good."

Of course every man knows how to handle a situation like that. First you start off by saying something about its being too expensive to own your own plane. Then you shut up and let the wife do the talking. If she's a good wife, within a half hour a man should have his plane. I must have gotten mixed up. Oh, I had my plane all right, in only half the normal time, but somehow a fur coat got mixed up in the deal.

By New Year's Day the deal was signed and delivered, and I must say my wife looked elegant. A few weeks later I had my plane. I took delivery during the biggest blizzard on record at the airport. For three weeks I couldn't even open my Christmas present, let alone play with it; but I had one consolation, my wife was warm and snug.

If my wife had given me another baby, I couldn't have been prouder. The guys at the airport crawled all over it. Her paint was as fresh as new and she had big German Gothic numbers on her fuselage, N666OD.

It took three weeks to dig the airport out. The runway was lined six feet high on either side with snow. It looked more like a tunnel. I climbed in, dressed in a suit as warm as a thousand-dollar fur coat. The guys pushed the plane out into position and George came over and said a few words to cheer me on. "Stop fighting your stomach; I know how you feel, but it'll all pass as soon as you start down the runway. Just remember that this ship has a big fat rudder and that's good for ground control. If you see yourself going for a snowbank, pull the release and kick the rudder." That's all I had to hear! Then he said, "Close your eyes. Where is the release?" I automatically reached for it and touched it. I'd memorized the whole cockpit in bed. "You'll do fine," he said and went over to pick up my wing to start the launch as I fought to get my heart out of my mouth.

My breath was coming in short gasps. I was waiting for the bell to ring for round one. I'd had a dozen or so solos under my belt, but they were all in a plane that I'd gotten to know like a baby knows its mother. When the canopy was locked, I let out a sigh and for a fleeting moment had a tense feeling that I would come to learn was part of the sport. The sigh seemed to express the protective part of us that we all have. It's our mother's voice saying, "Now be careful, Son," and if we live to be a hundred she'll still be saying it. But George was right. The instant that plane moved I went to work and there wasn't time for ambivalence. Decision-making in a sailplane is like no other sport. You line your problems up and tick them off one at a time, but the difference is that you're working ahead and are ready for the second and third problem as you're working out the first. After some experience this is not as pronounced as it is the first time around, but that first time has to be performed as if you have no tomorrow. Because you might not.

I was moving down the runway.

The first problem was to use rudder to keep the ship going as straight as an arrow to prevent the fifty-foot wings from getting near the snowbanks. How sensitive would these controls be? Lift her off. Stick back. Gentle. You're up! If you drift, remember the snowbanks, but don't get too high or the towplane will have problems taking off. How much forward pressure on the stick is needed to dip down and help the towplane take off? She's up. All is free and clear. What's the plan for a towrope break at each hundred feet until five hundred? The towplane stuck her nose up and so did I. My eyes, my hands, my legs, my whole body was *with* that towplane. I concentrated to anticipate her every move. We were a team. A fast glance at the altimeter told me we only had a few more seconds and all rope-breaking problems would have been passed. Then I could start to play and slowly get the feel of the controls before I cut free. There's an excitement about flying one's own plane, and I took a few seconds before I dropped off of tow to enjoy the feeling. As soon as the "mother" part of me realized what I was doing, "she" took over and got me back to work. But I had another pleasure in store that I hadn't anticipated.

When the altimeter reached three thousand feet, I pulled the plug, watched that the towline sprang free, and put my plane into a steep right-hand bank as the towplane turned left. She felt great as I gently eased her back into straight and level flight and that's when I discovered the second pleasure—a white landscape below, as far as the eye could see. Its beauty startled me because I hadn't given it thought. I was so concerned with the snow on the runway, I must have figured that it was *all* piled there. It was the first time I'd seen snow from a sailplane, which is entirely different from a commercial flight. Yes, you are in the air, but in a glider the ground is a part of flight and now it was a blanket of white. As exciting as the first flight was, I had to take a moment out to enjoy the toyland below and the winter sky above.

The rest of the flight must have gone well because I'm here to write about it, but I can't remember any of the details. I'm sure I stalled the plane to get her feel, and the maneuvers that George taught me must have gone well. The landing had to be right down the slot of that snow tunnel because everyone congratulated me. All I remember was the Christmas scene, seen from my own white star.

By Easter we were good friends; we'd come to know each other like husband and wife. Somewhere along the way George said, "Hey, why don't you take your flight test and get your pilot's license?" I hadn't given it much thought because the only real advantage the license offered was it would allow me to carry passengers. Try that in a one-seater sailplane; lovers couldn't even make it. The real reason for putting off the flight test was that the examiner was Tony, George's dad. He was the father image around the airport. Owning the place and also being the FAA examiner made him a double threat. Any time I made a landing that wasn't what I considered perfect, I'd sit in my cockpit a second or so looking around to see if Tony might have missed it. I'd feel much relieved when I'd spot him with his back to me, fixing something or other. But when I'd go to leave the airport an hour or so later he'd stroll up and say, "Take the landing pattern slower and you won't have that trouble. You've got to *think* in this game." Then he'd walk away and I'd feel crushed.

Almost fifty years old, and I caught myself "Yes, siring" him all through the flight test. Dealing with an IRS agent couldn't be any worse. When the examination was over he hemmed and hawed and did a lot of thinking. All I wanted him to say was "OK, you passed." The answer didn't come and I felt the perspiration oozing. If I flunked maybe he'd send me to jail. Finally he gave his answer.

That night I called Frank Taylor on the phone to tell him that I was an honest-to-God licensed pilot. His response was great and he added, "Now you can take me up."

"Frank, I've only got a one-seater and you're not my type!"

Frank wasn't just a great editor for me, he was an enthusiastic listener. The day we sat at lunch and I told him of a five-thousand-foot climb I'd made he was as thrilled as I was. Then he dropped a bit of a bombshell on me. He said, "Why don't you go after your FAI badges?"

I must have given him a look that said, "How the hell do you know about them?"

Frank didn't wait for my question. He said, "I was at a cocktail party the other night and I told a pilot who flies sailplanes about our project and he asked me if you had your Fédération Aeronautique Internationale Gold Badge. I told him you were only a student pilot. He suggested that after you get your license you should earn the awards so the people who read your book will know you were an experienced pilot."

"Look, Frank," I tried to argue, "any good journalist could get the facts and write a damn good book on flying to the moon. That doesn't mean he's got to do it."

"That's true. But if he does, he'll outsell the Bible." He gave me a look that I knew meant business.

That afternoon I fired a letter off to the Soaring Society

and asked for the requirements for all the badges. I got the answer by return mail, and the book on sex looked more and more promising. Skimming down through the list of requirements was an item that said: a cross-country flight of 186 miles. Obviously that was a typographical error. On closer study I saw that the major badges were divided into three groups: silver, gold, and gold with diamonds. This was ridiculous. A couple of the requirements for the silver badge seemed reasonable enough, but free climbs of 10,000 feet . . . and then a little later I read where they required a 16,500-foot climb. They must be nuts! I was having a hard enough time just staying up. The 5,000 footer that I'd made was a fluke; it was luck. I went to the airport and asked George what badges he had. He answered, "None."

"How many hours in the air do you have?"

"Oh, about thirty-five hundred."

My forty hours looked like a wisp in a thunderhead. For the next three restless nights I argued with Frank. "Look, George doesn't have his badges. Ed Wilkinson, who's one of the best SSA instructors at the field, doesn't have even his silver. George Moffatt, who flies at our airport, has all his badges but he's also the United States Open Champion. What the hell do you want? As the saying goes, it takes blood to write a book, but you want the real stuff."

Each morning when I'd get to the office I'd reach for the phone to call Frank, but then I'd decide to wait and see if I'd come up with some better idea through the night. It never came.

I decided to sit down and take stock. OK, Phil Gilbert told me about the sport. Art Hurst took me for a ride in a trainer. I liked it and decided to learn to do it. I signed up and put down my hard-earned cash. I took my lessons and lost a lot of sleep. Gordie Lamb, with great patience, answered my million questions about the theory of flight—then told it all over again. I had really fulfilled my ambition in the sport, if it came right down to it. I could take a sailplane up and ride the ridge lift for hours. Didn't I enjoy the excitement of floating only yards away from the trees? The climb to five thousand feet in a thermal was an experience to remember. I'm sure I'd find more thermals like it. I could land the plane like an old World War ace and I'd even learned to toss my white silk scarf over my shoulder with a nonchalant air. What more does a man want?

I looked up in the Soaring Society records the guy named Lobe who convinced Frank that I should kill myself for the book. Fast-talking Mr. Lobe was a member of the Society, but he hadn't earned any of *his* badges; he was pretty casual with my life. When I started this, all I wanted to do was get up and fly like all the other guys. I wanted to do what George could do. Now they'd gotten me going practically to the stratosphere on oxygen and flying cross-country. How do you get the nerve to fly away from an airport? How do you know where you're going? How do you know where you're going to land? Will there be a *place* to land? Madness, sheer madness. A guy could get killed! This insanity needed a family discussion.

I called to my wife. "Olive. Can you come into the study. I want to talk to you about something."

When she appeared at the door she took one look at me and said, "What are you doing, writing the monthly checks?"

"Worse. I'm thinking about getting killed."

"Oh!" she said with a surprised look, "I had the same idea about you at the party last night."

"Come on, be serious!"

"Oh, but I was!"

I told her about Frank's discussion with that bigmouth guy Lobe. I ended it by giving her the bad news that I'd have to fly cross-country.

She answered, "So?"

"Damn!" I answered, "it's a plot! Everybody except my

insurance man wants me out of the way." I handed her the Soaring Society requirements for the badges and as she read I went on. "Baby, once you're in the air you can't stop and ask directions, and without a motor you may not get there anyway. You don't come down when you want, you come down when you come down. Suppose I don't have any place to land? Suppose it's all trees, streets, or a farmer's field full of cows? Even if I find a farmer's field that looks good, what can I tell from a thousand feet? What about telephone wires, fences, stumps, barbed wire? A guy could get hurt. You know when I fly at the airport I don't land most of the time because I want to. I lose the lift and I fall . . ."

"Excuse me," she interrupted. "That reminds me, I have a cake in the oven." Out she rushed.

Oh, how I wanted someone to say, "Don't do it. Even at your age, you're too young to die." A man ought to be able to depend on a wife for at least that. My wife seemed more interested in preventing a cake from falling an inch than me from falling out of the sky.

In a few minutes she was back with a very serious look on her face. Now I knew I was about to hear what I wanted.

"I've been thinking about it in the kitchen," she started. "The silver badge looks easy up until that cross-country. Why don't you start on those tests that you can do at the airport and in the meantime talk to some people who have gone cross-country. I read in that soaring magazine that there's a contest at Sugarbush next month. Why don't you go up there and meet the people and see what it's all about?"

That sounded reasonable to me. It was a good stall; it guaranteed me at least another month to live.

Then it struck me. "My God!" Olive jumped. "I've got the first leg of the silver badge with that five-thousand-foot climb I made! The barograph tracing, which is required as proof of the flight, is still in the ship."

The next day I cut out of the office early and raced my hot little car to the airport. George was reluctant at first to open the locked hangar. He muttered something about having a date and why didn't I come back during the daylight. With some fast talking I got the hangar opened. We pulled the trailer out, I removed the fuselage, and then made a beeline for the barograph compartment. There she sat, proof of the first leg on my silver badge. George made a motion to unhook and remove the instrument and I practically slapped his hand. Everybody knows that a trace on smoked tinfoil is very fragile until it's fixed. I wanted to be the one to handle this treasure. I gently lifted it out and carried it to the car headlights. I'd done a good job when I smoked the tracing paper with burning camphor. The carbon was still solid. The headlights showed a strong tracing. We could see where the recording arm made the upswing to what looked like over five thousand feet.

Ever so gently I removed the tracing from the drum and laid it on the ground in the light. Then I went to the toolbox in the trailer where I store all kinds of junk. I fumbled around, searching for the spray can of clear lacquer fixative. It wasn't until I ran back and sprayed the tracing that I realized I'd grabbed the can of spray detergent. I could have cried, and maybe I did when my tracing dripped itself off the backing. The whole thing turned shiny silver. Stunned, I looked up at George. His only comment was "You've been foiled!"

A few weeks later, on a day when everyone at the field was climbing to seven and eight thousand feet, I could manage a climb of 3700. I was more than satisfied when I landed and fixed the tracing three times. It was sent off to the SSA office in California and in return they sent me a mimeographed letter awarding me my first leg of the silver badge. They even printed my name in their monthly magazine.

It was all a little anticlimactic. Yes, I did have the page

of the magazine blown up by photostat and hung on my office wall, but even I realized that it was only a mediocre show. That day was one of the best flying days of the year. I didn't tell those who came into my office that any fool could have stumbled to seven thousand feet that day. Those who knew nothing about soaring were stunned to realize that I'd climbed that high without a motor. My boss was impressed and bragged about it at a business luncheon. I was a hero. I've never told them, but what actually happened was that I hit a thermal so strong it felt like someone had kicked me in the seat of the pants. I was whooshed up so fast that I wasn't sure what was happening. Scared, the adrenalin rushed through my body, and I had to use fast hands to keep myself upright. To put it mildly, I was relieved and happy when, near the top of that thermal, I was flung out of it. It took a few seconds to discover that both the ship and I were in one piece.

If the first leg of the silver was won by being half-scared to death, the second leg, the five-hour duration flight, was won by embarrassment.

It's only logical that if a man knows he's about to make a five-hour duration flight, he'll take certain precautionary measures. In my innocence, I had a second cup of coffee that day. Who would have thought George would radio up to me suggesting, after I'd been up an hour, that I should try for my five hours? The first two-and-a-half hours were a cinch. Then I passed three. It was now my longest flight.

The last two hours turned into disasterville.

When the strong thermal conditions of the day ended, George radioed up to tell me to run for the ridge that was just a stone's throw from the airport. The ridge lift was just barely able to hold me aloft. I was getting so close—only fifty minutes to go. I was working so low on that ridge that I could see all the pilots who had finished their flights sitting around the ground radio sipping gin and tonics. I wasn't thirsty: I had a severe discomfort. Between sips my liquefied audience was giving me encouragement to stay up. When they announced that if I made it they'd have two drinks for me, I almost had an accident. Did you ever hear of anyone trying to fly a sailplane with crossed legs on the rudder pedals? Try that in a coordinated turn.

When my five hours were finally, finally over, I deliberately made a landing so my roll-out was as close to the bushes as possible. Unfortunately, I couldn't beat all the guys and gals that rushed out to congratulate me. They came running with the two tall glasses. All I could do was hope that one would be empty.

The contest my wife suggested we attend at Sugarbush would bring me closer to the moment of truth. I took my ship to fly locally after all the contestants were off on their daily task. The real purpose, as my good wife suggested, was to absorb and learn as much as possible about cross-country flying. This was the Mecca. The best pilots in the East had assembled for a go at this rugged ski country. Just looking at it from four thousand feet above the airport was scary. "Keep Vermont Green" is the slogan of the state. They have no other choice—not even one little brown spot to set a sailplane down. How were these guys ever going to fly off across these "mountains of trees" and survive?

Jim Herman, the contest director, was very cordial. I told him I'd only come to watch. Me and my big mouth said, "Next year I hope to fly in the contest, but right now I don't have the experience." I had my legs crossed, this time for another reason . . . I hated to tell such a blatant lie. I wouldn't be seen dead, or I should say I might be, flying a sailplane across all that Vermont green. I came to talk the sport, not do it.

Jim invited me to the precontest cocktail party at the Sugarbush Inn. I was delighted. The inn was elegant and so were all the pilots and wives in their drinking clothes. The gathering was held in a small dark-paneled, friendly barroom. I was introduced around. Putting faces with the names that I already knew from *Soaring* magazine was fun. Steve DuPont, a most active member of the soaring movement in the U.S. Top U.S. pilot George Moffatt. Sam Francis, a real contender. Bob Buck, the senior TWA captain and author. Tommy Smith, always in the top ten. The colorful Gleb Derujinsky, the all-around sportsman who loved competition, who was to win this contest five days later. The party was festive, but I had to remember that I was there for a purpose. I didn't want small talk or even good jokes; I drifted around, tuning into all the conversations. Near the bar were five guys in earnest conversation. When one fellow started to use his hands as all pilots do, even I knew from across the room that he was describing a landing. I rushed over not to miss the touchdown.

Here it was, just what I'd come after. They were talking about getting into short fields. The speaker, whom I didn't know, was saying that slipping the plane into a short landing space made more sense. Bob Buck interrupted him to say that he'd rather fly a good landing pattern and use the dive brakes for altitude control. He continued that the slip should be only used as a reserve measure. "Oh," I thought to myself, "if I only had a tape recorder. No book has this kind of information." Then for a fleeting moment I thought of Frank Taylor and what goodies I'd have for him at our next lunch. While my mind was wandering in this useless abstract area, a few of the wives came over to break up the shoptalk.

That left me alone with the fellow who had been talking when I joined the group. He seemed very well informed and now I had a chance at him alone. Just as openers I said, "How do these guys get the nerve to go cross-country, especially in country like this? I'm scared to death to try it." He laughed. Then I went at him, and for twenty minutes he explained the theory of cross-country flight, navigation, reading land and sky signs for lift, speed to fly, and so much more that I couldn't assimilate all he was saying as fast as he was throwing it at me. The problem with the experts is they know their thing so well they can't put themselves back in the shoes of the beginner. I had him repeat certain parts by questioning him in such a way that I hoped he wouldn't think me too stupid. As an old reporter, I slowed him up and got the real dope from him. It was a productive session. I not only got information for my silver-badge distance flight but expert, firsthand information for the book. When I saw that I'd pumped him dry, I asked if he wanted a refill and signaled the bartender. With all he'd given me I could at least buy him a drink.

As we waited for the drinks I said something in an awkward way about our not having met. He smiled and put out his hand as we exchanged names; he was Rudie Stutsman. Before he took the first sip of his drink, he saluted me with his raised glass, as much as to say, "Thanks for the drink." I returned the salute with my upraised glass and said, "Good luck in the contest."

"I'm not flying the contest," he answered. "I only have thirty hours in the air."

Feeling a little sick, I changed the subject and asked him his business.

"Undertaker."

FIVE

The
Lesson of Sugarbush

AFTER A FEW MORE NIGHTS OF RESTLESS SLEEP LOGGED IN my book, I came to the conclusion that no one could say anything to me that was going to make cross-country flying come any easier. Talking to them up in Vermont didn't help, it hindered. Sam Francis, as great a pilot as he was, cracked up on landing and split his ship apart in some farmer's field. It was the off-field landing that had me uptight.

My wife was very helpful through this period. She never once mentioned that silver badge. Instead, she read aloud every flier that came in the mail announcing contests in our area. All of a sudden I became so busy in the office that I couldn't get away for any reason; I couldn't even have lunch with Taylor. Lunch these days consisted of Tums with an Alka-Seltzer chaser.

Knowing that I'd have to make a decision sooner or later, the later was getting sooner. One day when I was putting Alka-Seltzer in my breakfast coffee, Olive announced across the table dates of the mid-Atlantic contest. "Oh," she said, "isn't that interesting; the contest is going to be in Pennsylvania during our vacation. Since we're going to Philadelphia, why don't we take the sailplane down and go over and watch?"

I missed my mouth with the fork and answered with egg on my face, "What do you expect the sailplane to see?"

"I enjoyed Sugarbush," she answered. "We met some nice people."

"Does the sailplane have to meet them in Pennsylvania?"

She never answered, but the look that came across the top of her coffee cup said, "Either get on with this business or quit."

I cleaned my face and muttered into my napkin, "OK, but it'll be the first time I pray for a rainy vacation."

"What?"

"Nothing, Delilah."

We arrived at the Philadelphia Glider Port three days before the contest was to start. The drive down from New York was uneventful. We didn't speak, though Olive did say that she'd looked at a topographical map of the area and it looked like open farmland.

I grunted some sort of answer. That wasn't news to me; I'd secretly looked it up too.

Jim Althouse, who was running the ground operations for the contest, met us and extended a warm welcome. Bob Buck, whom I'd met at Sugarbush, was the first familiar face. He talked with us about the fantastic flying weather and said, "TWA weather people said that it looked sensational and no end in sight."

"That's just great!" I faked it.

"Oh," chimed in Delilah, "if it's that good I'm sure Dick will get his silver distance."

"Nothing to it," Bob said. "On a day like this he could get up to three thousand feet and tumble thirty-two miles."

I thought that was a bad choice of words for a guy who was an author.

Then Olive got into the act by asking a question that

wasn't very wifelike. "If Dick makes his silver distance, will the contest committee accept it without going through the SSA office?"

Keeping a smile on one's face while one's stomach is turning over ain't easy. She couldn't be serious.

The first day at the field was one of the great stalls of all time. Charley Coy, the young college boy we'd brought along to help Olive crew, drive, and put the plane together, was knowledgeable about sailplanes. After about an hour of giving orders to him to do different jobs, he turned to me and said, "Are you really going to fly? All the things you've asked me to do have already been done."

OK, so I lost that ploy. The next one was to announce that I'd better get in the air and learn the lay of the land, the airport's landing patterns, and check things out in general. Well, no matter how I worked it, that was only good for the rest of that afternoon. At least it got me off the ground alone where I could talk to myself.

Bob Buck was right. In spite of my prayers, the next day was perfect. Everybody was watching the sky, saying what a great day it was going to be. I kept searching the horizon for the sign of only a teensy thunderhead. At noon there was nothing else to do but put on my parachute; Charley helped me into the cockpit. Olive gave me a kiss as the canopy was closed; that usually gives me extra lift, so up I went.

The day was very uneventful—for them. I sat up there at five thousand feet debating which way to turn . . . back toward the airport or into no-man's-land. I floundered all over the sky trying to cut the cord. Slowly, a massive depression set in. Sure, my wife said she'd crew, and come and get me, but I couldn't remember how good she was at climbing trees.

That night I was discouraged. Everyone seemed to sympathize. Bob Buck told me this was the *big* step. Sure, I had no idea where I would land, what kind of conditions I would find, where I would end up, what the farmer might say. It wasn't just uncertainty . . . I was scared. True, I was only going to be going thirty or forty miles—and guys today are going to the moon—but this was to be *me*. In the middle of the night I became so disgusted with myself that I got up to hook up the trailer and flee home. When I started dressing, my wife said, "Get back in bed." I did, and awoke the next morning with indigestion. It was a very quiet breakfast. Charley Coy was very thoughtful; he talked about girls. My wife was extremely understanding; she said, "Don't worry, we'll come and get you. I'm a good tree climber."

One day to go before the contest started.

Early in the morning, pilots from all over the East started to arrive. Everybody seemed to get the word that I was trying for my silver distance and if I made it I'd join the contest. Bob Buck wished me luck. So did Ben Green, the U.S. number two pilot. Gleb Derujinsky slapped me on the back. Art Hurst shook hands solemnly. Even *I* was starting to get the feeling someplace down deep that this was going to be my day. Gordie Lamb came over and went over my charts. My plan was to fly to Applegarth.

"That's good," said Gordie. "Just stay out of this section of New Jersey once you cross the river. It's the Jersey pine barrens and there isn't a spot for miles to set down a sailplane." I marked that in red but I wasn't planning to go anywhere near that area.

I gave my white scarf a tug and walked to the sailplane.

I dropped off tow at fifteen hundred feet, not because I wanted to; I had to! A boomer of a thermal kicked me in the pants, smacking me against the canopy. Within six whooshing turns I was to cloud base, pushing things down and pulling things out to keep myself from being sucked up in. "O God," I moaned, "I'll go, but slow things up a little." Exerting extra care, to sound calm, I radioed in to hook up the trailer. . . . I was off.

I knew exactly where Doylestown was because that was

the town I had lingered over the day before, trying to make up my bloody mind whether it should be go or no go. Doylestown? I found it on my chart, marked off my seven miles of accomplishment, and headed east—I think. From Doylestown on, Pennsylvania was a Chinese puzzle and New Jersey was the moon. At one point I saw a mess of railroad tracks down on the ground; I tried to find them on my chart and couldn't; by the time I found the mess of railroad tracks on my chart, I couldn't find them on the ground. As I approached a river, I recognized it as such—which gave me renewed confidence.

I scratched up a thermal off a shopping area (it must have been a discount center because the thermal wasn't much of a bargain) in goodness knows what town and tumbled over the river. I needed the extra height because I don't swim well. I called in to my crew saying, "Going over the Delaware River, have no idea where." Trying to figure that out became fascinating; it replaced fear.

When I got into Jersey all the towns, factories, roads, monuments, *anything,* all looked the same. Nothing came across like they said it would when I took the FAA exam. I finally discarded the aircraft chart and took out a road map. I found a mark! I located a town that I had known as a boy; it was called Mount Holly.

Now I knew exactly where I was. I made some fast calculations and the results were exciting. I had to be stumbling into some sort of world's record. How was it possible on a forty-mile flight to be fifty miles off course? That was quite a feat, not only in navigation but geometry itself. I was shaken out of my higher mathematical stupor when I recognized that I was headed directly into the miles upon miles of flat, desolate Jersey pines, the exact course Gordie told me *not* to take.

I was prepared to die. I saw the Jersey pines approach as I flew over a town. I had to make a fast decision on the edge of that hamlet: to tree or not to tree.

If this was the moment that had me so uptight for weeks and weeks, I was too busy to give my fears a second of my time. I scanned four fields. The first had high wires and looked short . . . the next was in crops . . . a ditch and maybe barbed wire. The last was it. The marks of the mowing machine were still visible. At nine hundred feet I was in a perfect position for a full pattern to land into the wind from the west. With calm ease I went through my checklist as I noted my exact landing spot on the field—trees, telephone wires, fence posts, ditches, wet spots, roll of the ground—all was in order. On base leg I could see no problem. Dive brakes were extended to hold the glide angle . . . speed was kept up . . . all sounded well . . . over trees . . . more dive brake . . . wings level . . . reduce dive brakes . . . level off . . . hold it . . . hold it. The touchdown was easy. Wheel brake . . . and for a split moment I was poised still, with both wings up. I watched the right wing drop to the ground and it was all over!

I just sat there.

What a relief. What had I been afraid of all this time?

It was great. It was sensational! I opened the canopy and sat giggling, self-satisfied with me. I wasn't even out of the cockpit before the farmer drove up in his truck and asked, "Everything all right, Mister? Hey, where's your motor? You all right, Mister?"

I was still giggling.

He stood over me, giving me a hard, steady look. I stopped laughing. His mouth dropped open. I saw fear in his eyes as he looked into my cockpit. I looked down, following his gaze. Over my heart my shirt was wet and bright red. My first thought was "My God, I'm dying." And what a shame after such a perfect landing.

My red felt pen had leaked in my shirt pocket!

Caesar never entered Rome with more pomp and circumstance than my entrance back at the Philadelphia

Glider Port. Even I was slightly embarrassed to be carried around on Charley Coy's shoulders. I was tempted to send a wire to Frank Taylor: SILVER BADGE ACCOMPLISHED STOP NOTHING TO IT STOP.

My official observer, Gordon Lamb, went over my barogram, checked everything out, and shook my hand. I played it very cool, as if it all were just another triumph in a series of victories. Bob Buck also shook my hand and said, "Now you can enter the competition." I'd forgotten all about that. Me and my cool, triumphant ways. Now my troubles were going to start all over.

Next morning I went to my first pilots' meeting to get the briefing on the day's task. The contest director had written all kinds of weather symbols and navigation instructions on the blackboard that were as clear to me as Hindustani. From this Sanskrit I finally got the idea that they were asking me to fly to an airport called Grimes, someplace near Harrisburg, find the place, and fly back . . . some two hundred miles! I thought, "They must have been smoking something last night and didn't offer me any." With my "world's record" of fifty miles off course the day before—I'd almost missed the whole state of New Jersey—how would I ever pinpoint a spot one hundred miles away?

Olive and Charley both said to give it a go. Art Hurst, who was acting as one of the contest officials because his new plane hadn't arrived, said, "Don't worry about going into competition. You won't win but there's always somebody behind you." He was right. I found out in that competition that there always is someone behind *you*. That someone, I discovered, is me.

I took off and shortly radioed to the timekeeper that I was going to make a start. They radioed back, "Plane who just called. What are your competition letters?"

"This is Wolters, I don't have any competition letters yet!"

"OK, use the last numbers of your registration numbers."

I had to think that over. My plane had N666OD painted on its side. They were printed in big German block letters. The 6s were more like Gs. I opened my radio and called down. "Ok, this is G–G–G–GOD and I'm going to start."

Some officious official on the ground sneered back, "The rules say you can only use the last two letters."

I figured I had enough problems at the moment so I decided to fly my ship, but who in the world would want to go around in the air known as OD . . . odd. I recognized Gordie Lamb's voice on the radio; he said, "Dick, why don't you use Old Dog?"

"Great!" came the reply from my ground station.

Later Gordie told me why. Old, because I was. Dog, because of the five dog books I'd written. I argued O for Olive, my wife, and D for Dick. Art pooh-poohed that idea saying, "A contest is serious business; Olive and Dick all over the air sounds like a love scene from a B movie."

Contest flying *was* serious. I went through that first start gate as GOD but I must have created a wrong turn on the way to Harrisburg. When Billy Penn, the statue on top of Philadelphia's City Hall, loomed up before me, I immediately knew an important navigating fact: I might possibly be flying east instead of west. With calm assurance, I made a 360-degree turn.

This was all very frustrating for me because I had just put a $500 radio into my new plane and now I couldn't even use it. I listened and was hearing such things as: "Gulf Lima, Gulf Lima, go to position number twenty-one" (that was Gordon Lamb telling his crew in code what to do so his competitors would be fooled); "Charlie Item, Charlie Item, get to the middle of the triangle" (that was Gleb Derujinsky giving his commands). Ben Green was also giving instructions to his crew. Oh how I wanted to get on my radio, but what was I supposed to do—open my microphone and say, "Old Dog to ground, Old Dog to ground; help, I'm lost"?

I finally made a navigation decision. Philadelphia is on two rivers, as any schoolboy knows. The big one is the

Delaware. I could tell which one was the big one. That pleased me. I flew up the other one, the Schuylkill River. I started to get over familiar territory, coming to a town I was sure was Pottstown—I think. So, I was now on the Schuylkill River at Pottstown. At last, I could let the world know I was in the competition. I proudly got on my radio, opened with my competition numbers, "Old Dog to ground, Old Dog to ground," and in my excitement wrongly announced, "I'm flying over the Susquehanna River, just east of Bethlehem." The Susquehanna is one hundred miles west of Philadelphia, and I don't think Bethlehem has a river going through it. But I do live on Susquehanna Road today, accounting for that part of the error; I guess subconsciously I just wanted to be home. Bethlehem must have come into my mind because someplace inside I must have figured I was getting close to God. My poor ground crew. They just looked at their charts: the guy upstairs had gone nuts.

I flew up the Schuylkill, finding thermals here and there, getting rather low. I at least had landing spots now. So I flew until I came to a big ridge that was filled with no landing spots, again. I gained a little height, and looked over that ridge and saw a few houses; as I got higher, I saw more houses; higher still, I saw a whole damn city over that ridge. Then I noted a big double-lane highway leading out of that town. I was elated to make a discovery! I found the highway. My chart told me this town had to be Bethlehem. Now I could follow the road out to the airport, Grimes Airport.

Goodness only knows where my ground crew was at that time. We hadn't been in radio contact for ages. I took that road. I later found out the town wasn't Bethlehem, it was Reading; that road wasn't going toward Grimes, it was heading south or east, and taking me back to Philadelphia!

I soon learned something about heavy weekend road travel. The bumper to bumper traffic below was giving off so much heat that I could float on the hot air over the highway. I flew over the Interstate at five hundred feet and went about fifteen miles. Something terrible must have been happening down on that double highway. The crazy cars scattered to the side of the road as I went along. They sure are terribly unsafe down there. As the road went down, I went down; as the road went up, I went up. When the road started to make a steady climb and appeared to be coming up to meet me, we parted. There was a field. I dumped it in for a good landing.

The farmer's wife offered me coffee. For the record, that was the worst coffee I have ever had in my life. I found, between slurps, that the name of her town was Plowsville. I'm positive it got its name because they stir their coffee with a plow. My wife came, thanked the farmer and his wife for taking such fine care of me, and she took me home. Her thanks to them disturbed me; but her coffee's not too good either.

The next day was not a very eventful day for me—at first, that is.

Carefully I picked my time to go up, took off, and was down in eight minutes . . . a meet record. I had landed, off-field at Rosenberger Airport, thirty-seven telegraph poles or two miles from PGP. I figured that I had done my day's work. I had made an off-field landing and that's quite an accomplishment. I sat in the cockpit waiting for my crew to arrive. My crew is always prepared; they had sandwiches, cold drinks, cake, so now I was ready for the better part of the day.

When they arrived, they frantically jumped out of the car. Charley madly started stripping the tape off the wings. My wife demanded that I get out of the cockpit. With bolts flying, they started taking that plane apart, making sure that I helped. They worked with a frenzy. I had no idea what they had in mind. Possibly, I figured, there was an early party starting back at the field. Then I thought it was a very

strange way for a crew to be acting, since I was supposed
to be the captain of the ship and with the ship goes the
crew. They hustled that plane back into the trailer, shoved
me into the back seat of the station wagon, sped down the
highway, got back to the field, took me back to the starting
line, and insisted that I help them put the ship together.
When they demanded I go back in the bushes to wee-wee,
I realized they were going to send me off again. Did you
ever see a sailplane pilot put his ship together with tears
running down his cheeks?

Actually, that flight turned out to be one of my best
flights of the contest. I was off and flying at about five
thousand feet after an uneventful, dry-eyed takeoff. A good
thermal, and there I was at cloud base. I headed down the
highway, following Route 309. This time my crew was determined they were going to stay under me and not let me
out of sight again. I radioed where I was, and they radioed
back, "Never mind using your radio, fly your ship!"

I thought that was a rather disrespectful attitude for a
crew to display toward the captain. I straightened out my
white scarf, stuck out my chin, and flew toward Carbon
County Airport with true competitive determination.

I must say that the night before this took place, Gordie
Lamb sat down with me, took out a chart, and showed me
exactly how to navigate. He said such things as, "See, that's
north and that's south." He pointed out a lake on the chart
and said, "See that little blue thing? That's a lake. Now
when you come out of a thermal, head for that lake. When
you reach that lake, pick out another lake, head for the
second lake, and that way you always keep your direction
in mind. Use your compass; don't just come out of a thermal, spin off and go. Fly from lake to lake!" I thought that
this made good sense, and the first thing after the task for
the day was announced at the morning pilots' meeting, I
got out the chart and looked for lakes on my course. There
were none!

During this flight I used my compass, and very shortly I

was crossing the Pennsylvania Turnpike on this speed test. Yes, I was on course, but I was getting very low at the intersection of 22 and the Turnpike. I got so low that a farmer started to wave at me. I waved back to be friendly, because I was going to use his field, and was just about to do so when I picked up a thermal and up I went to four thousand. I stuck the nose of the KA–8 down and went seventy mph ahead. Speed was the thing for today, but since I was bucking the wind, I was almost on the ground in ten minutes. I picked up another thermal and really went up fast, but unfortunately drifted back on the wind. There I was, going over that same farmer's field, and he was still waving at me. That maneuver took one half hour. I flew ten miles with no gain—another first for the record book.

But with chin out I went ahead again and did make some distance. On my radio, I was encouraged to hear Gleb say to his crew, "OK, let's start again." I figured he hadn't gotten away from PGP. I was ahead of him! Later I learned the truth. He was going around the course the second time.

Twenty miles ahead I saw a high ridge with a big hump on it. I headed for the hump, wishing it were a lake. That was the course I was going to have to take. Before I got anywhere near it, though, I was down looking for thermals. I flew over an orchard—the most beautiful apple orchard I'd ever seen. I got lower and lower and lower over this orchard. I got so low I could see each apple. It looked like it might become a real problem of geometry. How would one put a fifty-foot wing of a sailplane between those beautifully regular twenty-five-foot rows of trunks? It wasn't quite necessary, though, because I did get a good boomer at the last treetop second and thermaled up to six thousand feet.

Later when I landed I asked my landing witness, J. Winthrop Schildwasser, about that big beautiful apple orchard. He said to me, "That's no apple orchard—them's cherries."

Anyway, I got a thermal over the cherries and it took me

up to six thousand feet. Then I dove for that hump on that ridge. As I passed over it, I gasped, then cheered the news to my crew. There was "my" airport—my first-time-ever turn-point. In my excitement, I opened the radio and said, "Old Ground to Dog, Old Ground to Dog. Coming on the first turn-point." Oh, how I wanted to scoop the words back from the world. To add to my embarrassment, Ben Green opened his radio and barked back at me.

I went on past my turn-point and started photographing it. Again I got excited, and because I figured I might never see a turn-point again, I shot up the whole roll of film. When I saw the treetops in the viewfinder, I started to whistle "Nearer My God to Thee" . . . *please.* Since I've come through very weakly all my life, He did the same. I only made a few hundred feet and called another airport two miles away on my course. "I may have to land," I said.

They read me and came back saying, "Sorry, the airport is closed."

I called back and said, "Sorry, I may have to land." There was no other place near. They finally gave me the instructions and I landed.

The reason the airport was closed was that half of it was being taken up by a county fair. Needless to say, I got into the fair gratis. Having a sailplane come in was quite an event for Lehighton, Pennsylvania. The newspaper people were there almost as I landed. They were asking me all sorts of questions. My years as a reporter warned me I was going to be trapped before the interview started, but I forgot one thing: To hold my shoulder-length hair out of my instrument panel, I was wearing a tennis hat with my name Dick embroidered on it.

"Where did you fly from?" came the first question.

"Ten miles on the other side of Quakertown," I answered.

"All the way without a motor?"

"Oh, yes," I answered nonchalantly. "It's a contest for some of the best pilots in the East." I thought that was a rather clever way of telling them who I was.

One reporter turned to the other and said, "Hey, we've got a story!"

That clued me. He was a beginner; the other one looked like the sly one.

The sly one asked, "What's the name of the event?"

I told him.

"Who's in it?"

I ripped off a bunch of the guys' names. The only one he recognized was Steve DuPont, but it turned out to be another flying member of the famous family that he knew. I was, of course, waiting for the "trap" question that would be asked, "How are you doing in the contest?" I wasn't about to tell them last place. When the sly one started asking personal questions I was ready for him—I thought.

"Where are you from?"

"New York."

"How are you doing in the contest?"

That was the big question. With ease I answered, "First place."

"That's great," and then asked, "What's your name?"

"Gleb Derujinsky," I answered, because he was in first place.

"How do you spell it?"

God, that one I wasn't ready for. "Well, D-u-r . . . No, D-e-r-u-j . . ."

"Whose hat do you have on?" the sly one interrupted.

"Oh, that's my wife's," I quickly answered.

"Wait a minute," said the sly one. "Let me see if I have this story straight. You've flown this motorless plane over fifty miles?"

"Yes."

"You are in a contest and you're in first place?"

"Yes."

"You have a name you can't spell. You have long hair. You're from New York. And . . . and you have a wife named DICK?"

SIX

My Son the Pilot

I WAS RIGHT. I NEVER DID GET TO SEE ANOTHER TURN-POINT in the full five days of flying that contest, but I was all over the Pennsylvania sky. To some extent, things started to come together. On one flight I actually knew where I was every inch of the way. On that occasion I called it so close that I knew if I could manage to get over a ridge I'd find a river and a small town. When all this came to pass I was so pleased with my newfound skill that I photographed the town on my competition turn-point cameras, just for practice. Of course I seemed to know where I was, but my crew had a few problems relating where I was and where I was supposed to be.

When I landed in a field where a farmer and his dog were taking their afternoon stroll, he became so excited that he ran to the house and phoned every member of his family to get over to his farm fast—while the dog held me at bay. They brought friends, babies, grandmothers, dogs, cameras, and a pie. I was the local hero, and me with my long hair was a happening. Of course I'd lost radio contact with my ground crew, so I phoned my position back to the gliderport. There must have been a mixup, because after the farmer's family went home I was still waiting. At suppertime I was invited to join the farmer and we had a feast. After dinner I helped do the dishes, then went out and milked the cows. At dark I put out the cat and sat by the window waiting to see the headlights of our car come down the lane. I sat there wondering whatever happened to all those farmers' daughters I'd heard about. Besides, I was sorry I'd be missing the best part of the contest day—that one gin and tonic I allowed myself while flying. With my luck, I'd landed in a field where the farmer was too old to have any daughters at home and he was a teetotaler. I went five hours before my drink arrived.

I was enjoying my new position as a contest pilot. Actually, there were very few who went into competition. My silver distance flight was my ninety-ninth time in the air, even counting the endless number of training flights I'd had under George. It was obvious that cross-country flying was separating the men from the boys. I can truthfully say that every pilot in that contest was genuinely interested in my daily progress. They all had good advice, answered my questions, and told me things I didn't even know to ask about. This was a fraternity I enjoyed.

Bob Buck, at the evening campfire, told all of us about his recent TWA flight to Germany where he saw the first of the latest, hottest, fiber glass, standard class sailplanes coming off the assembly line. It was like someone sitting and listening to a full description of one's future wife. I knew I had to have her. That night before I went to sleep, I broached the subject to my crew chief, first mate, and present wife. When I finally had the nerve I said, "Should I order the plane Bob was telling us about?"

"Certainly," she answered, in a surprised tone. "Bob was telling me about it yesterday, I told him to tell you . . ."

"She must be a beauty, but no matter how lovely I'll

never let her replace you," I said lovingly.

"I hope you learn to fly as well as you talk," she said before going to sleep.

Back in New York I had all kinds of things to tell Frank. My silver badge #1496 arrived from the SSA and I wore it on every lapel I owned, including my pajamas.

"Frank," I said at lunch, "I ordered the hottest competition ship made. It's going to arrive in New York in ninety-three days and three hours."

He frowned. "Three hours. What's the three hours?"

"I've got it all figured out. It arrives in ninety-three days by boat, and if I get to the pier by 8 A.M. I'll have it through Customs and all the paper work finished by 3 P.M. It is just noon now, isn't it?" I looked at my watch.

I filled Frank in on every detail of the contest and he seemed as excited as I was about my new thing. "Frank, this is an interesting situation. I have about a hundred and ten flights under my belt and just the other day one of the instructors at the field introduced me to a friend of his. He said, 'This is Dick Wolters, known as Old Dog,' then he added, 'One of our competition pilots.' It's such a joke, but I love it. You should only know how scared I am between the pilots' meeting where they give us the day's task and the moment the plane starts down the runway on tow. Once the plane moves all the fears seem to stay on the ground. Now I know what a boxer goes through until he hears the bell for round one. I've also found out at this contest that I'm not the only one; most competition pilots go through this. It's part of the excitement of competition. Boy, wait till I get that new plane. I'm getting plane number two in the country. I can't wait."

But I had to wait. I put a calendar behind my chair in the office. Each day I'd mark off the day. But that went too slow, so I added a calendar over my bed: two marks seemed to make the time pass faster.

Then it happened.

At that time I was working as an editor for *Business Week* magazine. It's a good publication, and it would have to be a rather unimportant piece of business news that would get past that bunch of editors. I was sitting in an editorial meeting, and that's just about all I was doing. From my calculations I figured that at that moment my sailplane was being put into a container in Hamburg and with luck I'd get a telegram saying the ship would leave that night. I daydreamed about what my problems for the next ten days would be. What were the chances of a fire at sea? Could the ship be sunk by an old mine? FREIGHTERS COLLIDE IN HARBOR was a headline I was doodling with my pencil while our labor editor, Ed Townsend, droned on and on about some strike or other starting Saturday night. Ed, a real smart guy, had a way of talking that would put you to sleep even if his subject were sex. On labor problems he was positively anesthetic. He was saying, "Well . . . I think it will happen . . . I've been talking to some people and my . . . well, my guess is that Saturday night . . . well, yes, it'll take place and the whole East Coast will be tied up . . . but now, on the other hand, the President may . . ." Ed stopped and thought. "The longshoremen . . . well, I don't think they'll pay any attention to him and they'll strike." That's when I woke up.

"They can't strike! They absolutely *can't!*" I exclaimed, right out in the meeting.

Ten heads, twenty eyes, and the boss's open mouth stared at me.

Ken Kramer, our great editor, only called me Mr. Wolters twice in the twenty years we worked together. The first time was the day he hired me and the second occasion was when he slowly said, "Mr. Wolters, why can't the longshoremen strike?"

"My ship is coming in," I muttered.

"So is mine," he said drolly and turned to Ed and added,

"If they won't listen to the President, should we send Wolters down to the docks to talk to them?"

That strike was the longest in history. The terrible part about it wasn't the bloodshed and fighting on the piers; the worst part was that the *Hamburg Express* steamed up the Hudson and dropped anchor in the middle of the river, just off Pier 96 at Forty-second Street. My office, on the thirty-first floor, on West Forty-second Street, gave me a ringside seat. For fifty-seven days I watched through binoculars and tried to figure out which container might be mine. Ken Kramer called me Mister once more. He happened into my office one day while I was at the window with my eight-power glasses trained on the ship's deck. "Mr. Christian, are we becalmed?"

I never worked so closely with anyone as I did with Ed Townsend. I knew every move the union made before the rank and file got the word. The shippers were being unreasonable, and even editorials in the paper were telling us to write our congressmen before our economy was upset. I wrote Senator Javits and told him I didn't give a hoot about the economy, but my weekends were being ruined. I reminded him that my plane was sitting in the middle of the Hudson and I only had two months to get it ready for the Sugarbush contest. He never even replied!

Christmas that year came on March 1. The longshoremen and shippers kissed and said nice things about each other. I had my own words for both, but by 3 P.M. I had my plane and decided that I'd forgive and forget, too.

What a beauty! It got a lot of attention because it was the first one to fly in the East. Guys from all over the country called to see how I liked it. Now, with about 120 total flights under my belt, I became an expert. Even the maker wrote in a broken accent to ask how I liked my Libelle. Instructor George patted it, and Frank Taylor came to the field to see my first landing.

She was like a fine lady, oh so sensitive to the touch. I'll remember some of those early flights as long as I live. The day that Gleb, Art, Gordie, George Moffatt and I rendezvoused by radio and then flew twenty miles back to the airport in formation was the day I knew I was accepted as a safe pilot in the air. We flew close formation, with Gleb as squadron leader. Everyone at the field heard the radio chatter and waited for us to appear. It was a thrill for me to watch even as I concentrated on position. We came into view over the field, wing tip to wing tip. The ground radios started telling us how beautiful we looked until Gleb told them to shut up. The high-speed 120 mph pass over the ground went like clockwork. On the second pass, Gleb ordered Art and me, who were on the outside of the line, to chandelle to our outside and drop down to land short. George and Gordie made fast pull-ups, then outside turns while Gleb looped between them. He had all the timing worked out as the five of us were lined up in perfect order for landing in sequence, one over the other.

All this was making me a local big shot around the airport, but it wasn't doing a thing for me as far as making me feel any easier about cross-country flying. Actually, a new dimension was developing to my fears. Any time you landed in an unprepared area like a farmer's field, you were taking the chance of a mishap. How could I as much as put a scratch on my beautiful bird? That became a new worry.

With the Sugarbush contest only weeks away, I practiced all kinds of obstacle landings at the airport. I was practically landing on a handkerchief the weekend my parents came to visit. I'd said very little—actually nothing—about my flying to them.

You don't have to be Jewish to be a Jewish mother, but in my mother's case it helped. I figured it was better to say nothing than to have her get upset about my flying around in the sky. How could I really explain an airplane without an engine to an eighty-year-old mother who wouldn't let

me climb trees as a boy? At fifty I was still her baby. I called
on an old friend, Gene Hill, to give me a hand with my
parent problem.

Mother, who hasn't been slowed up one bit because she
is confined to a wheelchair, was rolled by Gene to the edge
of the runway. We placed her opposite the spot where I'd
make my touchdown. Next to the wheelchair we rigged a
portable two-way radio. Before the confusion and flak
started, I took off. Gene stood by her side and took over.

"Now, Mother," he said assuringly as I was towed aloft,
"watch his plane and you will see him release from the
towplane."

With pursed lips, she nodded and rocked back and forth.

"There! See that? He just released. Now he's flying on
his own. Isn't that beautiful."

She rocked back and forth harder. Her jaw was set.

"See him turning?"

No response. Her head was pointed straight ahead. Only
her eyes were tilted up. She wasn't going to give Gene any
satisfaction. Finally Gene said, "Mother, isn't he great!"

She broke her silence with, "He's only doing this crazy
thing to scare me. Let me talk to him."

Gene pressed the microphone button and put it in front
of her mouth. "Sonny, do you hear me?" she hollered. "Do
you hear me?"

"This is Old Dog, I read you," I answered. "How do you
like it, Mom?"

"Stop that Old Dog stuff and you come on right down.
Right now!"

"Everything's all right, Mom."

"You heard me. Now!"

"I'll be in soon."

When I'd glided down to about one thousand feet she
was able to get a close view of the plane. She turned to
Gene and asked, "Doesn't he really have a motor?" Now
she was looking up and watching every dip and turn as I
kept the plane directly overhead.

"How does he do it?" Then she said slowly to Gene, "I was so happy when he was a boy. He was the only one in the neighborhood who didn't go airplane crazy." Her eyes filled up and she said, "Now this."

"Now, Mother," Gene said, "he's really good at it. It's very safe. Isn't the ship beautiful?"

"Yes, it is. It must be beautiful . . . but don't tell him I said it. How does he do it? Where did he learn to do that? His father never did anything like that. How does he do it . . . and no motor?"

"Old Dog to ground. Mom, sit tight. I'm going to come in for a landing."

"Watch him close. He'll touch down so easy. See him starting to descend?"

"He's coming down the wrong way!" She called, "Shouldn't he be over here? Oh, my God, what's he doing?"

"No, Mother," injected Gene, "he's coming down, but he'll swing around over those trees and then land right in front of us."

She grabbed the mike. "Be careful, Sonny."

"OK, Mom." I clicked the switch to signal Gene I couldn't talk. I was in my pattern.

Silence.

Gene says that Mother became fascinated. Her eyes were glued to my approach. She held her breath as I cleared the trees at the end of the runway, watching me holding her steady for a touchdown opposite her wheelchair. When I touched down, her face lit up. The smile was from ear to ear. Then she did something she hadn't been able to do for years—*she stood up*. She stood up and put her hands over her head and clapped . . . and clapped as hard as her old hands could let her. She turned to Gene, and with tears of joy streaming down her cheeks she exclaimed, "THAT'S MY SON THE PILOT. THAT'S OLD DOG!"

SEVEN

The Sugarbush Contest

DRIVING INTO THE MOUNTAIN COUNTRY OF VERMONT BROUGHT
the old fears back. Trees, trees, trees—where does one set
a sailplane down in this country? What in the name of God
was I doing to myself? This wasn't the flat farm country of
Pennsylvania, this was ski country. Charley Coy kept saying,
"Don't worry, it has to look better from the air."

I caught that phrase, "has to"; even he wasn't sure. What
drives a man? I remembered a line an old friend, Jack
Randolph, once used in one of his columns in *The New York
Times*. "What is it that makes people crawl and claw their
way up the side of a mountain and then think they have
made a monumental accomplishment when the ants climb
up and down a rain spout every day and think nothing of
it."

The wonderful thing about Sugarbush was the welcome
one received. Jim Herman made me feel as though the
contest couldn't take place unless I entered this year. When
I tried to tell him that I brought my plane but wasn't too
sure if I could fly his country he said, "Come on, I'll spin

64

you around the course in my Aztec and you'll see that it isn't as bad as it appears from the road."

The plane trip did two things. It proved that I was right. Yes, there were landing fields, but they were miles apart. The plane trip also trapped me into saying I'd fly the contest. After he'd been so nice to me, how could I refuse?

The first contest morning Charley Coy had the ship ready, and when it came time for breakfast he was smart enough to talk about girls. I couldn't eat. My stomach was tied in a knot. My legs were shaky as I climbed to the roof of the tower where the pilots' meeting was held. Most all the faces and names were now familiar, and I did my best to greet all my old friends without showing how scared I was. I took my place on the bench next to Gren Seibels, the great competitor from South Carolina. Out of the corner of my eye I noticed that he kept opening and closing his charts of the area, fussed with his pencil, wiped his glasses, wiped his brow five times. He fidgeted all over the bench. Finally I turned and looked at him. He put out his hand and said in a warm Southern tone, "I'm Gren, I know you're Old Dog and I'm glad to know you—I guess."

"Well, Gren, you seem as nervous as I feel."

"I'm not nervous. *Hell,* man, I'm scared. Did you drive through those mountains?"

"Don't worry, it has to look better from the air." I repeated Charley Coy.

"Has to?" He caught it too. "You're not sure either."

I laughed a false laugh and took his wrist and placed his hand on my gut. "Want to feel the baby kick?"

That seemed to clear the air until Jim started the meeting. He announced that a movie crew was going to document the contest for a full-length feature film. With a smile he added, "If any of you are going to crash, could you please try to arrange it with Bob Drew, the director of the movie."

Bob stood up, took a bow, and added, "We have a heavy

schedule shooting with six cameras and crews, but . . ." He
took out a clipboard and read down a list; then he added,
"We seem to have an opening in our schedule about three
P.M. for the first crash."

Everybody laughed. But my gut started kicking.

By the time I took off that day I was a wreck, but the
moment my plane started moving down the runway, all was
clear. I'd come to discover this as a marvelous feeling. I was
ready for action—and it didn't take long coming.

I was off tow at the designated point over the golf course,
which is in a bowl snuggled close at the foot of the famous
ski slope. It was a gorgeous sight, but such thoughts had to
be pushed out of my mind; I was in business now and made
a few shallow turns looking for my first lift. I made a few
more turns. More turns. Then I moved over to my right, a
little closer to the ski slope and made more shallow turns
looking for my first lift. I was losing a hundred feet a minute
and *still* looking for my first lift. A fast calculation told me
that one hundred feet of sink would have me on the ground
in twenty minutes if something drastic didn't happen. It
did!

I got into three hundred foot of sink, and another fast
calculation told me at that rate I'd be down before the
towplane got back to the field. I remembered what Jim
Herman had told me. "If you get into trouble run for the
fire tower on the east ridge. There's always a thermal
there."

I stuck the nose of the plane down and headed across the
valley. Sure enough, a whole flock of sailplanes were working the "house thermal." By the time I reached it I was
below the ridge and already fighting for my life. A glance
at the field showed my towplane was just landing. Above
me the guys were circling like crazy and going up. Below
them I was circling like crazy and going down. Someplace
on the ground that thermal had to be kicking off lift. It was
like trying to find a needle in a haystack and I was getting

low—low enough to be doing just that. I searched every haystack in that valley until some of them were higher than I was. A glance at the panel clock indicated I'd been flying all of eight minutes. Making it back to the airport, only two miles away, was now out of the question. I was about to make my first off-field landing in my new ship. I radioed my intentions to my crew, who hadn't even had time to have a Coke after the sweat they had of getting me into the air.

"Old Dog, Ground," I announced, "going down in Waitsfield."

The radio came alive with chatter. "Damn," came a voice, "I told you. Now move it on the ground, fast. We've got it from up here. Get to field number one!"

I didn't have time or the desire to try to figure what that was about or who it was. I went ahead with my landing plans. There was a field below stacked with the hay I'd been searching. One section was cut in the morning and there was plenty of room between the bales. I patterned the field and made a touchdown that was a spot landing onto "half a handkerchief." As I rolled to a stop, very much pleased with my job, but disappointed that I had no audience, the radio came alive.

"Beautiful landing, Old Dog. Done like a pro. Don't look up! We are just above you in the helicopter. Don't look up! We have filmed your landing. Will you please open the canopy when we tell you. Climb out slowly. Wait till we tell you." Then the voice said, "Ground crew, are you ready?"

"This is Ann. Bob, we're rolling and have the whole take from the road. Old Dog, now open your canopy and don't look toward the trees by the road."

I opened the canopy, a little bewildered. Above I could hear the whir of the copter blades.

Ann, the film director on the ground, said over my radio, "OK, Old Dog, climb out. Good. Reach back for your landing card and charts. Look the plane over to see that she is OK. Give the plane a pat. Good. Now look around to see

where you are. Start to walk to the farmhouse by the grove
of trees . . . don't look to the road where we are shooting
from."

Bob Drew's voice came over the radio from the helicopter. "Ann, start Ed Eurich's son across the field to meet
Old Dog and have Tom's crew take it from there."

Tom's voice came on the air. "Old Dog, the farmer's son
will start toward you; you walk toward the house. We'll time
him to get to you about thirty yards from us. A sound man
will move in close to you. Pay no attention to him. Don't
acknowledge that he's there. Talk to the farm boy only. Tell
him what you did. Tell him about your flight."

"Listen, Tom, whoever you are," I said into my mike.
"I'll start all this nonsense, but nobody has to put words in
my mouth and tell me what to say."

In a few minutes the filming was over and I went toward
the house to phone for my crew to come get me. There, to
my surprise, sat my wife and crew already waiting. I wasn't
sure whether I should be pleased or angry. How did they
know I was going to land in that field? How did they know
to get all the equipment ready, all the people in place, and
have my crew there. What about having the farmer's son
all primed to come meet me? How did they do all that and
my total flight time only eight minutes? I decided to play
it cool. I said nothing and asked no questions. Besides, I
was so pleased with that first off-field landing with my hot
ship that moviemaking was not the most important thing on
my mind at the moment.

The winner that day was Gleb; he got one thousand
points. I got fourteen, but I was pleased.

The next day was a whole new life starting. My belly was
just as upset as the morning before, but once I rolled down
the field I had my problems solved. I'd made my plan the
night before—I followed Gleb Derujinsky. I picked my
takeoff time right after his at the pilots' meeting. When I
got off tow I didn't search for lift, I searched for Derujinsky.

I found him and got on his tail. I let him search for the lift. Some smart, I thought as we climbed to over five thousand feet. He radioed the start line and announced that he was going to go through the gate, the imaginary rectangle in the sky. I announced the same thing and dove to follow— 90 mph . . . 100 . . . 105 . . . 110 . . . 120 . . . Mad, mad man!

"OK, Charlie Item. Good Start!" came the voice from the start line.

"Good start, Old Dog."

"Damn right," I answered.

"No chatter please," came the voice from the ground.

Gleb pulled up on the stick and I did the same. When my stomach and my plane met, we were back in our original thermal climbing back to five thousand feet. Now I understood the reason for the fast start. The trade-off of speed for altitude would get us back to the place where the thermals were. Gleb flew out of the thermal and headed toward what are miles and miles of trees. "OK," I thought, "if he's going to do it I'll do it too." He was a half mile ahead of me and he was hitting some heavy sink. He started to fall out of the sky like a lead balloon. I held back in a small thermal and sat in it to watch him disappear almost to the tops of the trees, but still he drove on. "What gut!" I thought. When I lost sight of him he had to have turned back to the airport and landed and taken a re-light. I decided to make my own plan. To get to Rutland, over the worst mountains in Vermont, I'd use my head. With my altitude I could fly across the tall range that was the ski slopes and out into the Champlain Valley, down the outside of the mountain chain . . . and have safe landing spots all the way. It looked like a great idea, and I was about to beat Gleb.

I headed west to get over some of the worst terrain in the state. At six thousand feet I had no worry, but whatever it was that pushed Gleb to the deck hit me too. I fell out of the sky so fast that I didn't know what hit me. Within minutes I knew I wasn't going to make it across the mountain. In another minute I realized that I wasn't going to make it back to the field. Things were happening so fast that one by one my options vanished. I was trapped with only trees below and in 1000-foot-a-minute sink.

I pushed the plane for all I could; I raced at 120 mph to get out of the downdraft, turned to try another direction but the down air stayed with me. Now, below the mountaintops, I was working too hard to be scared. I had one last chance. I headed north toward a spine coming off the big mountain. If I could reach it and get over it, I'd be able to make the golf course in the bowl and land. The only way it could be done was to dive for the base of the small ridge I had to cross, then at 120 mph pull up, trade off the speed for altitude, and reach the safety of the other side.

I dove, pouring on the speed. I was below the top of the spine heading for the trees. They zoomed at me. I held my fire until I could make out the branches and then pulled back slowly on the stick. Up went the plane; all I could see was sky. I leveled off as my air speed read sixty. I made it up and over the top by forty feet. There, in front of me, were oceans of lawn. Never again will I belittle the golf player. May he turn all the woods into golf courses!

I was so relieved that I hardly remember the landing.

Drew was on the radio as I touched down. "We got that from the air. Beautiful save. Will you wait for the ground camera crew? We had your landing spot picked out wrong today . . . sorry."

"Hey!" I shouted over the radio. "I want to talk to you."

In the meantime I ran into another problem. My landing gear made a divot, if that's what the golfer calls a hole in the turf. The greenkeeper came up in a golf cart and was as mad as a wet hen about what I'd done to his green, which I had to admit was now partly brown. He gave me a hard time and gave my crew a worse time when they drove over his course with a car and trailer. As I drove out with the plane safe in her bed, his parting words with shaking fist were, "And don't you ever come back and play this course again!"

That night I talked to Bob Drew, the moviemaker.

"Bob, how did you pinpoint my landing that first day?"

"Well," he said slowly, "making a movie is very expensive. We can't be all over the state of Vermont with crews just waiting for a pilot to happen down in a particular field, so we took a look at the entry list. We knew that you were new to this game and we zeroed in on you for this part of the film. We took a look at an air chart and figured that we'd get you in one of three fields." He smiled. "We hit it on the nose yesterday and only missed you by ten minutes today."

"Bob, yesterday I got fourteen points, today twenty-one. Gleb now has two thousand. How am I going to do tomorrow?"

"You're going to do fine."

He was absolutely right the first day, almost right the second, and dead wrong in his prediction for the third.

With my mere thirty-five points out of two thousand, I wasn't very happy. That night Charley was again talking about girls and I was seriously telling my wife that I was real upset because I broke the soaring pilot's cardinal rule—you never allow yourself to get into a situation where you need luck to get you out of it. Sure, I had shown a certain amount of skill and, even more important, I learned that in a tight spot I don't get rattled, but I was doing very badly. I couldn't seem to stay up.

I knew I wasn't about to win any contest, but I also knew I was a better pilot than my 35 points showed. The third day I was out to prove it. The task was to Lebanon, New Hampshire, and return. The weather was not the best but it could be worked slowly. Picking the early afternoon for my takeoff, I was in the air working the weak lift over the fire tower at about 2 P.M. At 3 P.M. I was still grinding around in the same thermal, just holding my own at 3000 feet above sea level. The airport was 1470 feet ASL and the ridge to the east another 1200, so I wasn't too high. There must have been 25 other planes in that same thermal. That is an experience. We all circle the same direction, but at times the planes are only yards apart. It's precision flying, and extreme care must be taken. An hour or so of that will have one as rigid as a pole. I made my plan. If I could inch my way up to 4000 feet, I'd go off on course. Oh, how I wanted to get out of the Sugarbush Valley. For two days I'd been trapped in it. I felt confident that this was going to be my day. Hadn't Bob Drew told me so?

Time goes slowly while circling in a gaggle.

Then all of a sudden things started to happen. Slowly I was going up and holding the gain. Some of the fellows had gotten discouraged and flown off to find greener pastures. I could see a lot of sailplanes were landing at the airport. At 3800 I had the feeling I'd make the next 200 feet and I'd be on my way. At 3900 I radioed to the crew to hook up and get on the road. Charley Coy answered the transmission. "Good boy, Old Dog. Tonight I won't have to talk about girls."

I could see the sky starting to recycle. Should I go or wait awhile? Something inside said "Go."

I taped the altimeter when she pointed to 4000 and banked the plane and watched the compass swing to 164°. I held the speed at best lift over drag, 53 mph. Over and out of the valley I went. A road in another valley below showed me the way.

Sam Francis was on his radio to his crew. He was going to move out but he said, "Go to hill." I knew what he meant. He wanted them in a good position so they could stay under him, but he was waiting for the conditions to improve. Should I have waited? Five miles out on course I hadn't felt a bump of a thermal. I moved over to the high ground. There *had* to be a "house thermal" over here, too.

Following Gleb hadn't done a thing for me the day before, so I decided my decision to go it on my own was the best way.

East Braintree passed under my ship. I followed the valley below and saw a rock cliff off to the left. "That's where my next lift will come from," I half-sung to myself. Trying to find it cost me four hundred feet in altitude. No luck. I flew on. The valley was falling away at about the same rate as the altitude I was losing as I went on my way toward the "big" town of Randolph. "I'll get some heat off the buildings," I thought. When I arrived the sun blotted the town out, and I ran for the high country. I ran for the big factory in the center of town. A sick feeling edged its way up through my body. I'd made a glide of twenty miles.

Sam Francis' radio announced to his crew, *"Go!"*

I announced to my crew, "I'm in trouble at Randolph."

"Hold on," said Charley. "I don't know any more girls to talk about."

I could have cried. This wasn't the end of life, but I'd built it up to be so. How I wanted to get back to Trux Pratt's chalet that night and at the dinner table tell the story of my magnificent flight. Didn't I have the best plane in the contest? What was wrong? Sure, I was scared of cross-country flying, but I was trying my best and, even more important, doing it—but oh, so badly.

I might not have had to land at Randolph, but I'd let my mind wander to these discouraging thoughts when I should have been working on a low-altitude save. There was nothing else to do. I picked out a landing spot, flew low, right over the houses, and touched down in a field that was perfect. I rolled up to the road to make things easy for my crew.

I sat there a long time before I opened the canopy. What was I doing wrong? Three days of flying, my total time in the air was less than two hours, and over an hour of that was in one thermal over the field. How could I write a training book about soaring if I couldn't even stay up? At that moment I looked up. At about four thousand feet I saw a sailplane going overhead toward Lebanon. What was he doing that I didn't know? I was going to radio up to see who it was and then decided not to. The hell with it!

"Old Dog," my radio spoke. "Sorry you're down. Your crew is about eight miles back. They'll be there in fifteen minutes." I recognized Sam's voice. I didn't answer. I just clicked my mike in recognition of his call.

A car drove up the road and jammed on his brakes, kicking up dust all over the place. Before it had come to a full stop the driver was out. He didn't even bother to close the door. He ran across the field toward me as if a bull were chasing him. Still running, he started, "I saw the whole thing. I heard you fly over the office and I was out like a shot. I saw you swoop over town and come in for the landing. It was beautiful."

I just nodded. I wasn't in the mood to have to start to talk about no engine and how great it must be flying on the wind.

"What a story this is!" he added, all excited. "Can I take your picture?" Out came a camera. "Sorry, I forgot. My name's Jackson. Bill Jackson. I'm the publisher of the Randolph *Gazette.* Ha. Ha. Editor, too. You got here just in time. I'm putting this week's issue together right now. Got about forty minutes to get the story done."

He started pointing a camera and clicking away. I still hadn't opened my mouth.

"Where did you come from? Do you have a pencil? I ran out so fast to see what all the whistling noise was. That's when I saw you pass right overhead. Sure is a beauty! Where did you say you came from?"

"New York," I answered.

"No, I mean where did you fly from?"

"Sugarbush," I reluctantly told him.

"All the way over the mountain without a motor. Why

that's a good twenty-five miles. You must be one of the great pilots to do a feat like that. Do you mind, I'm going to do a feature piece on you. What's your name?"

"Don't write this up," I tried to say.

"Boy, what a front-page feature! We haven't had anything like this for a long time. What did you say your name was?"

"Dick Wolters."

"Look, Dick, I want to tell my readers all about it. I only have a few minutes. I've got to get to the shop and close the edition. How does it feel to ride on the winds as free as a bird—carefree and with grace and silence?" He was writing his own story, his way. Without stopping, he continued, "Mr. Wolters, you have to be one of the great pilots in this country to do such a feat without an engine."

That was the second time he pulled the great pilot bit. "Look, Mr. Jackson. Let me tell you something. This was the lousiest flight I've ever made. Don't write that great pilot stuff in your paper. I'm flying with twenty-five other guys in this contest and I'm in last place and not only that . . ."

"Come on, Dick, you don't have to be modest with me. I know a real story when I see one. Why, my brother-in-law has a plane right here in town and he couldn't fly over that mountain and all the way down this valley without a motor. Come on now, you have to be an outstanding pilot."

I was getting fed up with his chatter. "Look, the guys I'm flying with will do a hundred and fifty miles today. I failed badly. I'm so damn sore about it. If you write me up as a great pilot you're going to be making a fool of yourself." I was just about ready to blast him for giving his readers the garbage he wanted to write when I caught sight of a sailplane just overhead. I looked up and saw the competition letters on the tail, RB. His landing pattern looked good.

"Mr. Jackson, here's your story. He flies the Atlantic every week in a 747. He's TWA's senior pilot. At the age of sixteen he flew solo across the whole U.S. In that day it was a great feat. He's got all kinds of awards and . . ."

"Dick, excuse the interruption but I've got to get to the office and write this and get the pictures developed. All you say about the other guy might be true, but it only proves my story. If he's the world's best, as you say, your flight was exactly as long as his. That makes you one of the great pilots. We'll leave the world's best for the big city papers. You won't feel slighted if I only call you one of the country's best. That's big enough for Randolph, Vermont."

And off he ran to his car.

Bob Buck rolled his plane up to mine and opened the canopy.

"For being one of the world's best pilots, you didn't get very far." He frowned as if he didn't understand me. "I hope you can drive a 747 further than this."

"Look, Old Dog. They built the 747 to go a long way; they put twelve toilets aboard." Out he scrambled and ran for the bushes.

The next day, the fourth task, taught me something about the sport of soaring that I hadn't anticipated—*there is a hidden cost.* It all started when I was at about three thousand feet over the Sugarbush Inn, working a weak thermal, and sensed a different smell to the air. The wind had shifted to the west, visibility was noticeably better, and some clouds were popping over the east ridge. I radioed down to my crew at the field, "Hook up the trailer and move out." That didn't cost anything; radio megacycles are free.

The first leg of the triangle was again Lebanon. I felt a lot better this time when I reached Randolph; I was four thousand feet over the newspaper office where the press was printing the hot news of the great feat of the day before. Southeast of Randolph the conditions started to deteriorate. I held my cool and started searching for the elusive lift. I worked everything that looked as though it might produce updrafts, chased wisps that I hoped would turn into cumulus clouds only to have them dissipate before I reached them. Flying around wasn't the hidden cost—my fuel was free. When I got to East Bethel, I got the feeling that one gets what one pays for.

At South Royalton, the river makes a bend. The ridge faces the northwest—salvation! I'd get on the ridge, fly it, and wait for the sky to recycle. No sweat, I thought. I had landing fields by the dozens below. Great farm country. I picked up some speed, flew on the ridge. I decided that I had one more ploy—heat emanating off the buildings in South Royalton. I swung around the ridge, made a fast pass right over town. My ears were listening for the song of my variometer signaling lift. Nothing happened. I'd have to land. My eyes picked out two good fields. At pattern height, all was well.

I pulled the dive brakes over Third Street. The gear was put down. I raced back over the checklist—wind . . . pattern . . . trees . . . wires . . . posts . . . rocks. I couldn't have asked for a better crop; the hay wagon marks were still in the field. With dive brakes whistling, full out, my downwind leg was right up Main Street.

The touchdown was fine, the roll-out short. When I took off the canopy, I heard a strange wailing noise but paid no mind. Within seconds it all came back to me. I couldn't believe my eyes. Racing across the field, going lickety-split, came the South Royalton fire department in full regalia. Ten men in assorted gear: a few helmets, a few pair of boots, some raincoats, axes, ladders, hose, buckets, and whatnot all piled on a brightly painted red jeep, with forty arms and legs bouncing cattywampus right at me. We must have appeared equally mad to each other. There I was— wide eyed, stunned, motionless in my cockpit with my water bottle halfway to my lips—openmouthed, catatonic.

The guy with the most gear on, except for one boot, jumped off just before the contraption skidded to a halt, one foot from my wing tip. He ran at me with ax in hand, stopped short at the cockpit, and bellowed down at me, "Y'all right? All right?"

I managed some sort of nod of my head. In minutes, all was well. I explained that I had not crashed. They were fascinated with my sleek fiber glass Libelle (No motor? And it could fly over the mountains?) I never had such a willing ground crew. A rope was attached to the ship and the little red fire engine pulled me up to the road, aided by twenty wing-walking arms.

Now comes the hidden cost.

First, a case of beer from the local pub. Off went the jeep to fetch it. When it returned, with it came the cars of every man in the company, and their wives and kids came too, to see the plane crash. The little red jeep with proud gold letters, SOUTH ROYALTON FIRE DEPARTMENT, NO. 1, on her stern was sent off for pop and ice cream. This time when it returned it came with its twin, fire engine No. 2—another little red jeep with the identical assortment of people and parts.

My expression of disbelief was soon answered by the chief—the one who was still in only one boot. "Well," he twanged, "when the siren went off we knew we had two emergencies, a plane crash and a brush fire. So we just split up, half to each."

The hidden cost was just doubled to twenty bucks when the second batch of women and kids arrived; the little fire engine went for the pop.

Then it dawned on me. One fire engine had come to the "plane crash" while the other went to put out a brush fire in town. "Brush fire in town?" I questioned the chief as he drank my beer.

"Yep," he guzzled, "right in town."

"Holy cow!" I exclaimed. "How could I have missed that when I flew over? If I'd have seen it I could have used the heat it gave off to take me up and I'd still be on my way to Lebanon."

"Zat so?" He raised his eyebrows and thought a minute. "Glad you didn't see it. We ain't had a fire company picnic like this since last Fourth of July. The kids is havin' fun." He showed four missing teeth before he guzzled again.

I at least had a fun story to tell that night at the dinner table at Trux Pratt's chalet, which he called the Pratt Fall. I told them, "If I fall out of the sky tomorrow, I couldn't afford to have it happen in South Royalton again."

But that's exactly what happened!

The task for the last day of the contest started off with the first turn-point Lebanon. What the second point was, I don't remember. It's not important since I never made one turn-point in the whole contest. I seemed to have been right back in Pennsylvania when I shot the whole roll of film at my first turn-point with the thought in mind that it could be my first and last. Flying down the valley toward Randolph was just a milk run for me. I knew every inch of the way that far. From Randolph to South Royalton was easy to navigate, so this time I concentrated on finding lift. Sometimes when you look for things too hard you can't find them if they're sitting on the end of your nose. I even checked there and it wasn't around.

I kept following the river until I was low enough to get on the ridge that flanked the north side of the town, hoping as I had hoped the day before that there would be enough wind from the north or west to give me ridge lift. I was barely able to hold on for a few passes. I was afraid to go to the far edge of the ridge—I didn't want anyone in town to see me and have them blow their damn fire whistle again. On the other hand, I might be missing another brush fire. Getting lower and lower on the ridge, I knew I had to make a move fast. This time, instead of making a pattern over the town, I flew straight over it to land on the other side. As I went over Main Street I saw the red jeep pull out of the firehouse. With that, I banked hard right to get out of sight and made a straight-in landing on a farm near the river. I glided to what I would have hoped was a distance outside the legal limit of the town. In my haste I forgot to look for any brush fires, but at least I was happy to save the price of another fire company picnic. I prepared to set my lovely bird down in a field where a farmer was driving his tractor in circles, or whatever farmers do. I flew in, touched down, and rolled out within ten yards of him. As I did so, I remember saying to myself that I'll bet he hasn't had a thrill like that since he was in the big city.

I opened my canopy and sat watching him. He couldn't have missed seeing me. He didn't even turn his head, and round and round he went. I couldn't figure it. A sailplane coming in for a landing, right in your field, isn't an everyday happening. I even had a landing later in my career as a pilot, where my approach surprised and excited a woman sunbathing on a blanket so much that she stood up to watch as I came closer. She forgot she was nude, but I wasn't one of those barnstorming rowdy pilots; I made my first touchdown with my eyes closed.

This farmer didn't blink an eye, turn his head, or lift his foot from the gas as he drove his machine right on past me, making his row upon row. Thank goodness, I hadn't landed in the area where he was plowing!

There was no use waiting him out. I climbed out of the ship, took my papers, and walked toward him to ask if he'd attach my line to his tractor and get me out by the road. On his next round I waved to him to stop, but stayed clear just in case.

"Hi," I said with my most friendly smile. "I just landed a plane in *your* field."

"Ain't mine," came the sour reply.

"Could you give me a hand and . . ." That's as far as I got.

"Look, mister," he said, "I got to get this field done by night. I don't know what that thing you got is, but let me tell you, you landed on the meanest farmer's place in these parts." With that he hit the gas and was off.

That's all I needed, farmer trouble. Then I remembered something Gordie Lamb had told me. If you get with a bad farmer, talk to him about his farm. That will soothe him. I walked toward the big house, stopping first to read the name on the mailbox. I saw some movement by the barn. At the door I called in. "Mr. Appleby?"

"Yes," came a voice. I couldn't decide whether it was friendly or not.

A big guy came out into the light, wiping grease from his hands. I knew my long hair wasn't going to help matters, but I used the most friendly face I could muster up and added a bit of a drawl to my voice. "I'm Dick Wolters. Could I use your phone? I'll pay for the call. Got to talk to some folks at Sugarbush." I thought that "folks" would get him.

He thought about that as I sized him up, and he was doing the same to me.

"Come to the house" was his only reply.

We walked in silence until I stopped and surveyed his whole place. He stopped, too, and turned toward me. With my best Southern accent and with my arms crossed I said, "What a fine spread. Looks just like my daddy's place in Virginia." Well, that wasn't a terribly big lie. My wife's daddy did have a big farm in Virginia.

"Yes, sir, just like the hill country in Virginia."

"You a farmer?" he asked.

"Well"—I strung that "well" out—"well, not really, now."

I walked toward the fence to get a better "look" at his place.

"What do you grow on your place?" he asked in a friendly tone.

God, I couldn't even think of things they grew on farms down there. "Oh, we grow all kinds of stuff . . . watermelon . . . ah, corn . . . cotton." With that I thought I better get on to more familiar ground with him, so I squatted down,

sat on my heels in true farmer style, picked up a handful of
dirt and let it slip through my fingers and said, "You sure
have good land here. Fine soil." Then I added the real
country touch. I swung my hand out, pulled on some green
stuff and stuck a piece of it in my mouth and started to
nibble on it.

I looked up at him with that thing hanging out of my face
to see if he was ready yet for me to tell him about my plane
down in his pasture. I noticed a strange expression on his
face.

He said, "I wouldn't do that."

"What?" I asked.

"Put that in your mouth."

"Why?"

"Poison ivy."

That was the end of the Sugarbush contest for that year.
Bob Drew's movie was started there and finished later in
the year in Texas, where he recorded the story of Gleb
Derujinsky making some gutsy flights and George Moffatt
going on to become the national champion. Another thing
was started at Sugarbush that year and it became a tradition
for many of us for years to come, the hospitality and fun of
Pratt Fall. Needless to say, my poison ivy story brought a
good round of laughter at the big square dining table that
sat in the middle of the main room.

Trux was a warm host. His house was primarily for skiing
and it had loads of bunks and beds on the second floor that
were used each spring for us soaring pilots. The only real
dues one had to pay to be part of this group was to help
do the cooking, dishes, and all those things—and be a good
sport. You had to be able to razz a guy about his flying and
also—very important—to be able to take a razzing if it was
due. One night at dinner Gordon Lamb told in perfect
German accent the story of the soaring pilot who went up
in his lederhosen to fly in a contest. By mistake he took the

car keys with him. His wife radioed up to tell him the keys were in his pocket. The guy, to save the price of a second tow, called down to her and said that he'd put the keys in a handkerchief, fly over the field, and drop them. All was set for his pass over the field. He counted to three on the radio, threw them out of the cockpit, and asked her if she saw the handkerchief coming down.

She answered, "Nein."

Of course the next day you know what happened to Gordie. He was halfway to Morrisville airport when his most beautiful, dignified wife, Anita, who was crewing for the first time, got on the radio and said, "Gordon, where are the keys?"

There was a long silence . . . no answer.

Poor Anita, who had never worked a radio, got right back on the air and said, "Gulf Lima, where are the keys?"

All kinds of hooting and howling came over the radio from the other members of the Pratt Fall gang.

Trux came over the radio to Gulf Lima ground and said, "Vell, dey es most likely in der lederhosen." That brought a lot of guff from all over the sky.

Cool and collected, Gordie called down after a long period of time when he must have been searching his pockets. For a guy six feet three inches tall, strapped in a parachute and a sailplane cockpit, searching pockets would be quite a feat. "Right, Gulf Lima. I have them, but there's another set in the hide-a-key box."

"In the what?"

Poor Anita had again forgotten that all her transmissions were supposed to include her pilot's competition numbers. "Excuse me, Gulf Lima, in-a-what?"

At that point in the contest, when the planes were being launched, all the pilots wanted to reach their crews to give their instructions, all on the one channel, and the start gate was having its problems too.

"In a little box . . ."

The transmission was interrupted by the call to the start gate.

"Yvxct un . . . one half mile from the start gate."

The start gate radio came on saying, "Pilot who announced one half mile out please identify yourself, we are having a key problem and your transmission was garbled."

"Gulf Lima, I didn't understand you. We must have a party line." She was frantic.

Finally Jim Herman, the contest director, got on the radio and said, "Will all pilots hold up communications until Gordie and Anita find their keys."

Now the air was clear.

"Gulf Lima to the ground."

Anita quickly answered. "This is Gulf Lima ground."

Gordie said, "You don't have to answer every time I say Gulf Lima."

You could hear the tears about to burst when she answered, "You told me to do that."

"Wait for my message" came a peeved voice from the sky.

Silence. Neither now knew who was going to speak and they didn't want to be talking while the other was talking and miss a message.

"We're waiting," said Jim Herman.

Gordie came on. "The extra keys are in a little black box under the hood."

Relieved, Anita said, "I read you, Gulf Lima."

"OK start gate. Thank you, pilots" came Jim's voice.

The radio was all a-chatter with the stored-up messages. Then came, "Gulf Lima, how do you open the hood?"

"With an ax" was one reply.

"Gulf Lima ground, under the dashboard there is a knob. Pull it."

"Gulf Lima," said Anita, "that's a stupid place for it."

"Gulf Lima ground. When you get the hood open, you'll find the hide-a-key near the ge-xzz-ator."

"Oh, Gordie, someone cut you out," she said in a cracking voice.

"Near the gen-er-a-tor," he repeated clearly.

"I read you," she said in a happy voice.

"Competition pilots, please hold up. I think we now have the hood open" came a tired voice from Jim Herman.

"Gulf Lima. Gulf Lima! I have it open!"

There was a long silence. All ears were glued to their radios. Then there was a click. A microphone was opened. On came a small female voice which asked, "Gulf Lima . . . what color is a generator?"

Trux, a most elegant host, always gave a toast to anyone who was either sitting at his table for the first time or to anyone who had a good day. Needless to say, he had a toast ready for Anita and her Gulf Lima. With eloquent words he presented them with a three-foot wooden key to the car.

I'd been proud of my poison ivy story, but it came off in fourth place at that last night's dinner. Dinner was served late because we were all waiting for Art Hurst to arrive. Finally his car drove up and we watched from the window as he got out. There was something strange about his walk. His arms were out to the side and he walked with his legs wide apart. When he came in the front door, a terrible odor invaded the room. Art, always in Brooks Brothers clothes and immaculate—never even ever unshaved—hollered: "Excuse me!" And then he ran upstairs.

Boo, his great college-boy crew, got out of the car in only his jockey shorts. He was dripping wet and had to have been swimming. He came in the house laughing so hard he had to sit on the floor, lean against the wall, legs apart. His body shook. I wasn't sure after a moment or so if he was laughing or if he was hysterical. He tried to speak; it came out laughter. He was trying to say something but it wouldn't come out. Finally he said it. "My . . . my chicken-shit pilot." Then he collapsed into uncontrolled laughter.

We got the story out of Art when he arrived at the table
in a new, clean ensemble. He sat there a long time, then he
started slowly. "I can't believe it. I was doing fine. I was
getting over the Hungry Mountains near Stowe when I ran
into what had to be the down side of a wave. The whole
valley turned to down—six- and eight hundred-feet-per-
minute stuff. Just what you ran into the second day, Old
Dog. I couldn't get out of it, so I decided to fly it all the way
through the pattern at eighty mph—just to be on the safe
side, and thank God I did. Just as I was about to touch down
I saw a barbed wire fence. One of those one-wire things. It
must have just been put up because the grass under it was
cut like the rest of the field."

"Come on, Art," interrupted Trux, "get on with your
stinking story."

"Well," said Art, using his hands now to describe his
plight. "I pulled back on the stick and had all the speed I
needed to get over the wire, and in fact over the long low
building at the end of the field. I knew there was a good
field on the other side because I almost picked it first. The
reason I changed my mind was that it had a kind of blue
cheese look to it that I thought was strange for Vermont
soil. Well. I zoomed up and over the barn. The moment I
was over the building I could smell it was a chicken farm.
I panicked but didn't have time to pull up my landing gear.
I didn't touch down, I oozed into six inches of that . . . that
chicken stuff. It flew in all directions. But the worst part
was, it rammed up through the landing gear and sprayed
like foam all over me; the cockpit, the canopy went black
and I thought I'd gone under. My buckles were so slippery
I couldn't get out of the ship. I thought I was going to die,
but never dreamed I'd go this way."

"You've had a rough day," Trux said. "Come on, you'll
feel better with some food in you." He passed Art his plate
of chicken chow mein.

Art ran for the bar.

Near the end of the dinner Trux lifted his glass and I started to smile because with his wonderful gift with words, I knew he was going to tell us how he enjoyed flying with us and being our host that week. There was never a phrase in his speaking that even hinted a kind of stuffiness that most people express when they try to act out this role. "Here it comes," I thought—but I was wrong.

"All week I've enjoyed your stories," Trux started. "Now I have one."

We all applauded. "It better be funny," said Dan Starr.

"Judge for yourself" was Trux's fast reply.

"I was having the best flight of my life. I made the turn-point at Lebanon and was on my way to Morrisville. I was having bad luck on the east ridge, so I crossed over to the big range at Duxbury."

"Come on," said Art, "get to your story."

"That's fair," answered Trux, as he lifted his wineglass and saluted Art. "I'll get on with my crazy story. I had to land when I reached Waterbury. No other choice. I saw a big—I mean big—lawn. It was as big as an airport. Bigger than the Sugarbush airport. When I came over the fence I noted that it was one of those eight-foot steel mesh things with barbed wire strung along the top. I set her down in the corner of the grounds. When I got out there wasn't a soul around. At the far end of the property was a big brick building."

"I know the place," said Dan. "Did you . . ." He stopped and laughed into his plate.

"Well," continued Trux, "I walked at least a quarter of a mile to that building. In the front was a long flight of steps. Not a soul. Not a car. Nothing. I went to the steps and started up. The door was open and I went in to talk to the receptionist. There wasn't a soul around. The foyer was all marble and the place as clean as a whistle. There wasn't a sound. On either side between the columns was a hall. I looked down both sides; they were the same—doors all along as far as the eye could see. Well, I decided to go down one. I tried a door; it was locked. I walked farther and there I met a guy coming out of one of the offices. He seemed surprised to see me. I smiled and said, 'Can I borrow your telephone?'

" 'Well, I don't know,' he answered politely. 'Who do you want to call?'

" 'The airport at Sugarbush,' I answered. 'I have a crew that will come get me.'

" 'Oh?' he replied. 'How many.'

"He gave me a strange look," Trux continued. "I started to get angry and said, 'Damn, I only want to use your phone. I'll pay for the call. What kind of place is this, anyway?"

" 'Don't you know?' he answered.

" 'How would I know, I just flew in ten minutes ago.'

" 'You flew in?' he asked, questioningly.

" 'Yes, my plane is out back.'

" 'I didn't hear any plane,' he said.

" 'Of course not.' Now I was really getting sore," Trux said. " 'It doesn't have a motor. It's a . . .'

" 'No motor?' he interrupted. 'Where did you say you came from?'

"Lebanon."

" 'You flew all the way from Lebanon without a motor? Is that what you are trying to tell me?'

" 'Look! All I want is a phone,' I shouted.

" 'Please don't raise your voice,' he said quietly. Then he said, 'We can't allow you to use the phone without special telephone privileges from your doctor. You know the rules.'

Dan Starr, giggling, with his head almost in his chicken chow mein, said, "Wait till this story gets to Wall Street. They always said you were crazy. How did you get out of the loony bin?"

"Looking around this table, with all my friends," Trux answered slyly, "I'm not sure I did."

EIGHT

The Gold Badge, Some Diamonds, and Girls

FRANK TAYLOR AND I HAD LUNCH ON MY RETURN TO NEW YORK.
We had a lot of laughs over the happenings at Sugarbush.
When his chicken cacciatore was served to him, I told him
the Art Hurst story. He chuckled when he picked up his
fork, but he didn't eat much.

"Well," he said, to change the subject, "sounds like
you've become a pretty good pilot. When are you going to
take me up?"

"Why you old so-and-so. You've been waiting to see if I
was going to kill myself before you asked."

"Frankly, yes. Weren't you the one who said that you
could produce a fine how-to-fly book even before you knew
how? I fell for your line that a good reporter could write
a book on going to the moon even if he didn't do it. I waited
until I was sure that when *we* took off for the moon you
weren't going to be reading the book on the way."

"OK, let's go."

"Will you take my kids up, too?"

"Sure."

We met that weekend at the airport and I hired a two-place. His boys were all excited and wanted to toss a coin to see who went up first. I noted that Frank solved the problem by announcing that he'd go first. I turned to him and said, "It's interesting, in all species of living things how the parents want to protect their young."

Until we were in the air and flying around for a while, Frank was as tight as a drum. I explained in detail, as we flew, what I was doing. I could tell by his one-syllable replies and the way he was holding on to the cockpit that he was a little uneasy. When we hit a small thermal and I banked over to swing into it and start my climb, Frank came to life. He couldn't believe it—we were climbing on air.

"Watch the altimeter. The big hand will show you how fast we're going up."

He came down as excited as his boys, and the rest of the day was a delight. We made a lot of flights, and they fought all afternoon as to who would go next. When one of Frank's flights turned out to be a fast glide down because I couldn't seem to find any lift, he demanded another flight and his younger boy said it wasn't fair, he'd have to wait his turn.

Later Frank and I talked about the book. He said, "We're going to make the graphics of this book as handsome as the sport."

That's what I wanted to hear.

He thought for a moment and then said, "What's your next step? What are you going to do, fly more contests?"

"I think I'd like to fly the National Championships next year." I quickly added, "For the fun and experience."

"Could you do it? It sounds impressive as hell and would make good book jacket copy."

"Always thinking business." I shook my head.

"How do you get entered into such an event?"

"Hell, I'll tell them that I'll write it up for a magazine if they let me enter. No, seriously, I'd have to qualify. I'm sure even with the low scores I'm making in these sanctioned regional meets that I get some sort of points toward my national rating. If I can get in enough meets I should be able to make it. I also have to have my gold badge. The ten-thousand-foot climb I'll stumble into some day. It's that flight of almost two hundred miles that has me buffaloed. Fifty miles seems to be my limit before I start trying to kiss some farmer's daughter. Well, I've got a lot of time to think it over."

But I didn't have as much time as I thought. That night I got a call from Herb Jason. "Old Dog. Allan MacNicol is going to run his wave camp up at Mount Washington this year, why don't you join us? Bud Briggs and the whole Iroquois Club are going to go. It's the best place in the East to get your altitude climb and the gold is almost certain with the right weather. What do you say?"

I'd never gotten into a real big lee wave. It's entirely different flying from the heat-produced thermals. The wave is a phenomenon in nature that few know about. Air, like water, is fluid. When you sit by a stream and watch water pass over a rock and then when the water goes on down stream past the rock it makes waves, that's the same thing that happens to air. If a steady wind is blowing, at say thirty mph, across a flat area and then strikes a mountain range, the air will flow over it, but then behind the mountain it will make waves just as the water did behind the rock. The wave stays stationary in the water and it does the same thing in the air. If you float a straw down the stream it'll bob up when it comes to the part of the wave that goes up, and it'll go down when the wave goes down. If you watch closely you can see the straw climb up the side of the wave. If you flew a sailplane into the upside of the air wave, it too would climb. Unfortunately, we can't see air so we have to know what we are doing to be in the right place. The downside of the wave will be going down at the same speed as the upside goes up. There's one danger. Just as water will make eddies, and in a swift stream they can be dangerous, the air that races through the system also spills off eddies. They're called rotors and are violent air eddies made by air that does not turn and go back up into the wave system. Flying in the wave is like flying on silk, but rotors have been known to tear small planes apart in flight.

It's always astonishing to people to learn that sailplanes have gone higher than forty-six thousand feet on a wave, and that record will be broken when it's tried in a pressurized plane.

The cloud formation in such a system is also very interesting. On the upside of the wave, when the moisture in the air gets cold enough to condense, a cloud is formed. When the air continues up above that, it's dry. Then, when the air turns and comes back down, it will pick up the moisture again and carry it down. These clouds are the signal in the sky that a wave is working. They appear to be standing still because the front edge of the cloud is constantly forming at the same rate that its back edge is dissolving. They're known as lenticular clouds. The interesting thing for the soaring pilot is that there's always an opening in the clouds at the front edge of the lenticular cloud. The cloud system could be thousands of feet thick except for the "up" air that keeps that one area clear. Pilots call this opening the window. They climb up through it and can see down through it. When they're above the clouds, the window is their way back down. The rotor or eddy has its shape too. While the lenticular is classically almond shaped with sharp edges, the rotor is like a cotton ball and it pumps and fights like a boxer.

With all that clearly in mind I prepared for my expedition to Mount Washington. I took about ten hours of blind-flying-instrument training in a Link trainer just to have some idea what I would do if for some reason the system stopped and I'd be caught above the clouds with no window to descend through.

When I told Herb that I would certainly come up to try my luck, I had no idea that it was going to cost so much.

It cost me $134 to get outfitted with cold weather gear—but the check I had to write was for double that amount, $268.

I bought ski-doo boots with goose-down booties. My wife liked them so much that I bought her a pair. I bought a goose-down vest. My wife liked it, too, so I bought her one. Goose-down warm-up pants my wife liked, so I made it two. I bought a goose-down ski jacket. My wife . . . so I bought. Hell, I just ordered two pair of goose-down mitts. They only cost $28—no use being a cheapskate for a lousy fourteen bucks. But an even more serious problem developed: try to get into a Libelle cockpit with $134 of goose on. Feathers? Man, it must have taken a whole flock to outfit me.

Finally, Neil Hyslep preened me into the cockpit. I felt like a chicken about to be hatched, and that first tow was rough—with my vario chirping and cackling, I thought my yolk would bust. If you think that was a sight, you should have seen Bud Briggs.

Of course, you have to realize in Bud's defense that dressing for the wave isn't exactly like going to a formal dinner party. It's advised by those who have suffered the cold of twenty-five thousand feet to wear silk socks next to the skin, under the wool. I stumbled onto the information that nylon will do when I inadvertently walked into Bud's camper; he was sneaking and grinding into a pair of his wife's pantyhose. Embarrassed, his comment was "I don't have silk. Nylon's just as good, and if it'll keep the feet warm it ought to work for all parts."

I should have had an indication that the tow was going to be rough the night before when I arrived. Winds of over one hundred mph have been recorded at the weather station at Mount Washington, and when I pulled onto the North Conway airport with my sailplane in tow, Bud Briggs and Neil Hyslep were there to help me lash the trailer to the trees on the edge of the runway. I slept in my camper at the field that night and I rocked as though I were on the high seas. This is some rough country. The area can best be described as miles and miles of vertically rolling "farmland." The crop these farmers grow isn't exactly for food, it's trees for building houses; they also grow rocks—miles high.

I saw all this on the mandatory orientation flight that Allan MacNicol gave me in a Piper Cub. What a ride! I never did do well on horses, all that up-and-down motion was not very appealing. No horse could have stood this flight. My hat is off to the makers of the Piper Cub. My hat off and on, literally, as that little plane crashed through the violent up-and-down air action of the wave. Barreling through it vertically is like running into a stone wall. The country below was most unattractive for a pilot; the naturalists can rave all they want, but this would be my last choice in the world for a place in which to be forced down. When we got back to the airport, by following a blazed trail in the woods, I was undecided whether to cry or go home—or both.

The next morning I was up bright and early. In the dawn light the setting was magnificent. Mount Washington stood in the background in its full majestic splendor. We helped each other put the planes together and I did it with real care. I inspected every inch of my lovely lady; she might be in for a real beating.

The tow is the kind that is not described in books. No one could find the words to explain how you follow a small plane from the airport to the wave; the fact that you're attached with a two-hundred-foot rope seems to make no difference. Keeping the sailplane somewhere in the ball park took a new kind of yoga. We were both flung all over the sky, but the sailplane's long wings made it react with much more vigor. I was on top of the airplane, under it, out to the side—and in no special order. I was so pleased to think that before I took off for my first try that I'd had the sense to go around to all the fellows and say good-bye to them. I remember Herb's saying, "Come on, what do you have to lose but your breakfast?"

The only thing that kept me from losing my cookies was the thought of what I'd ever say to my dry cleaner. You simply have to use your imagination to know what it was like. At one point I got so sick that I turned on my oxygen and took a few whiffs. That seemed to settle me down; at least it kept me alert. The towplane turned and changed direction. I saw a rotor ahead that was ready to do battle. It was a beautiful sight—from our distance. We flew around it with me shoving and pushing everything to stay at least in the same county as the towplane.

Suddenly . . . suddenly, everything went pianissimo—silent, calm, lovely. The towplane wagged its wings, the signal that we were in the wave. I released and my audio variometer started singing the loudest song she ever sang. I took stock of where I was and checked all my instruments. Then I looked down and made an imaginary mark on the canopy as to where a road intersection and a ski lodge were. That was to be my mark; it should stay there through the whole flight. Above, the sky was bright blue up through the window, the rest of the sky was a dirty gray—cloud base. The most amazing thing, it was like flying on silk. My cockpit was as steady as though I were sitting in my living room chair. The wings were not rocking an inch: they were poised as a statue and going straight up at one thousand feet a minute. When I reached the base of the clouds it was a new experience. Below I checked the crossroad and lodge. They were at the exact same spot on my canopy. My air speed indicator was reading seventy miles an hour and I was standing in one place in the air—but, going up. When the plane entered the window, about half a mile long and one quarter of a mile wide, it was like entering a fairyland. I could have touched the wisps as they danced to a lazy tune. I was awakened from the dream world. "Old Dog.

What are you finding? Are you in the wave?" came from my radio.

"Going up through the chimney. I mean window, Herb. It's great, come on up."

"About to take off, Old Dog. Keep the radio on. If you hear two clicks when you talk to me, it means I'm reading you but not transmitting. Over."

I clicked my mike button twice to show him I knew what he meant.

Chimney was the correct word for describing this window. The walls were three to four thousand feet high. Where the sun shone on the feathery walls, they were white as snow, in the shade they were black; every tone of gray was in between. The effortless passage up and out into the open was magnificent. As I broke out I looked down and there was my road. It hadn't moved an inch on the canopy.

Being above it all was phenomenal; a tingle of excitement went up my spine. Seven thousand feet in a world of cotton. I looked to the right, left, ahead—white against a sky so deep with blue. I turned my ship to get a look behind . . . GOD WHAT A MISTAKE!

Instantly I was disoriented. Instantly from a view of hundreds of miles to nothing. Nothing! My brain raced. Should I turn and find the window? My eyes flashed at the turn-and-bank, the blind pilot's eye, and I remembered what I'd learned in the Link trainer. I set up level flight. I'd have to go down through the clouds . . . how thick were they? . . . Four thousand feet? How much clearance between the mountains and the clouds? . . . One thousand? Hold it steady, needle . . . ball . . . airspeed . . . needle, ball . . . airspeed.

It was scary, but the brain can't stop, when it's working with such fervor, to indulge in feelings. The beauty of such a situation comes later, knowing that you allowed your knowledge, limited as mine was, to take over. I do remember talking aloud to myself, reading off my instrument panel. I didn't ask myself if the clouds might have drifted below the mountaintop. If it had, I'd never have known it anyway.

With full dive brakes out, my altimeter unwound like a crazy clock. How long it took, I don't know. I can now calculate it at about four minutes. For an instant I saw ground below. It wasn't seeing the ground for that split second that got me excited. What made me shout out with joy was that the ground was *below,* not over my head or off to the side; *it was below.* I'd done the job as I was supposed to. I hadn't tumbled out of the cloud, I'd flown out. At the next burst of ground that slid across my canopy, I jammed stick and rudder opposite and practically flew out of the hole in the cloud, wing first. One thousand feet below was the top of Mount Kearsarge—as I'd hoped.

It wasn't all over when I broke out into the clear. I was still in the down of the wave, and going down at 1000 feet a minute. The top of Kearsarge was getting close, fast. I stuck the nose of the plane down and we whistled to safety out in the valley at 130 mph.

When the instrument panel sang that all was well, I realized that I was wet with perspiration and the thermometer in the cockpit was still reading below zero from upstairs.

I still hadn't had enough time to realize what I'd been through. I just sat out in the valley and flew around for a few minutes trying to decide what to do when the decision was made for me. My vario started to sing *up.* The ship took on that silky feel. Everything went soft and smooth. I looked up and there was my chimney again. I moved ahead about a half a mile and slowed up when the joy of the climb was screaming at me from the instruments. Up I went.

Five thousand, 5,500, 6,000, 6,300. The window was wide and its chimney walls were churning in the sunlight. Then, as fast as the eye can blink, and the mind can think, I was inundated in the gray darkness. A wave skip! I knew the instant it happened what it was. The "water in my stream" changed velocity and the window moved and left me engulfed. All I could think was "OH! NO! NOT AGAIN!" Then I figured "What the hell!"

Now, as an experienced hand at blind flying, I went through it all over again, but this time I had a worry. If the system changed, and I knew it did, did it move and engulf the mountain below? My eyes strained to pierce the grayness. It seemed an eternity before the grayness of mother earth filled my canopy. Kearsarge was only eight hundred feet below!

With dive brakes full out I dropped out of the grayness zone into the green world below, and this time I wanted it. The brakes were never retracted. I flew to the airport and landed. Herb was there to help me out of the cockpit. I was wobbly-legged when I managed to get me and all my goose feathers out. We didn't speak. He must have seen that I'd had quite a time. I walked toward the camper. Now it was all the heavy down that had me sweating.

"Let's have a Coke," I suggested.

"How did you do?" he finally asked.

"If that's wave flying, I don't think I want any part of it."

"Did you get caught in the cover?"

"Boy" was my only reply.

"Me too!"

I didn't want to talk about it too much because I wasn't sure if I was going to try it again. We had the Coke, relaxed, and had some lunch. "What do you think, Herb?" I finally asked.

"Well, it's what we came for."

Neil Hyslep joined us in the camper and asked how we'd done in the morning. Herb answered and told him his story, which was an exact duplicate of my experience. He also got caught in the overcast.

"Come on, you guys," Neil said after seeing that we were both a little hesitant to try it again. "This is some of the best wave condition I've ever seen. It could be years before you'd be lucky enough to hit another day like this."

Our decision to go was bigger than any of us could have known at that moment. While dressing in all our down gear, I told them about Bud Briggs and his wife's pantyhose. They were both laughing about it as we pulled our ships in line to wait for the towplane.

As we got to the line Herb said, "You go first, Old Dog."

"You go," I replied.

"You lead the way," he replied.

"I'll toss you." Of course, with all the gear we had on, no one could have gotten into an inside pocket for a coin, so I flipped an imaginary dime up into the air, watched it go up, down, "caught" it in my palm and turned it over onto the back of my left hand. Looking over to Herb, I said, "Call it."

"Heads I win, tails you lose. Look, you go ahead. While you're on tow I want to check out my radio connections and see what's wrong."

The tow wasn't as violent as it had been in the morning. I released at only two thousand feet over the ground, when I felt the first smooth lift catch my wings.

This time there was no problem getting up through the window. Breaking out on top at seven thousand feet was again a glorious spectacle. At eight thousand feet, with the cockpit thermometer reading zero, I was as warm as toast dressed in all my feathery down. That's when I wished I had a camera on board. A skein of geese—twenty of them—fell in line with me. It was a thrilling, magnificent sight as they moved into formation off my wing. Could they have smelled me as one of their family? As they took off, I thought, "Thank goodness, I wasn't down in those mountains wearing a bear coat."

At nine thousand the view was sensational, and at ten thousand still pegged at one thousand feet per minute up I prepared to put on my oxygen mask. As confident and cocky as Bogart in *Casablanca*, I reached for the oxygen regulator. I turned it—it wouldn't turn. I pressed it—not a budge. I didn't panic. I just ripped off both gloves and yanked, pulled, hammered. Stuck! A few choice words helped me, but not the regulator. At zero degrees I started to sweat. Would I have to descend? At eleven thousand I swore again, gave it one more try—*nothing.* Finally, I loosened my straps and scrunched down; then, picking my best three choicest words, I kicked the regulator with my knee. With the ease and savoir faire of Cary Grant I turned on the juice with thumb and index finger—as easy as holding a cup of tea—pinky held high. Smiling to myself, I took a drag of the oxygen to settle my adrenalin.

Did you ever try to put a mask on over two pairs of glasses, flying yellows and the reading variety that sit on the end of your nose? That's not too difficult for a baldy, but, with *my* hair, my first attempt brought it all down over my eyes. At eleven thousand I thought I was flying among the trees. When I finally reorganized all parts, I remembered the warning to check the oxygen, my reflexes, and feelings. I flexed my toes—they flexed. I blinked my eyes—they blinked. I wagged my wings—they wagged. I added two plus two . . . multiplied two by two and got six . . . and then knew I was in normal, fine shape, alert—on top of the world in all its meaning. I settled back to enjoy the flight.

That's when something happened. I can't describe it because I don't know what it was. It seemed to be some sort of uneasiness. I tried to forget it by looking down through the window at the crossroad and ski lodge below. It looked just as I had expected. I was thousands of feet above the lenticulars—free and clear . . . no problems . . . all systems go. But I couldn't shake the malaise. The view was stunning, the feeling strange. I checked the instruments carefully—the oxygen, the airspeed, forty-five mph. Was it the slow speed that seemed unreal? The height? A new perspective of the world? The silence? *Silence!* That was my clue. I tried laughing off the feeling. It didn't work. Instead, it seemed to spread up my legs and into my gut. Damn, I hadn't read about anything like this. Finally, I realized that I had to solve this one—fast. My brain searched. I knew I had to find the reason. I'd read about mental and physical problems coming on very fast at high altitudes. I tried to think of all the possibilities. Then it came to me: I was lonely! Simple as that.

At fifteen-thousand feet there were no cars to race on the highway, no kids to see in a swimming hole, no farmers down there waving up to me, no newspaper reporters to fight with, no trees to stick my wing into, to scratch and search for a breath of lift. I didn't need any lift. I had all I wanted, and that was a strange new feeling. Landing areas were the furthest from my mind. No calculations of distance were called for; charts weren't necessary while standing still. Was this soaring? Not as I'd known it for the past two years. At eighteen thousand feet I didn't have any problems. I've always had problems, always had something to solve. I wasn't people lonely—I was problem lonely.

How does a soaring pilot get used to looking down instead of up on cloud base? Once I figured this all out, and was ready to relax, I got my wish—a real problem. I thought I had heard myself laugh—the first sign of mental disorientation? Then I caught myself in an honest-to-God giggle. Tut, tut, Briggs in Joan's pantyhose. My brain raced . . . hypoxia? The giggle is the first sign of oxygen starvation. My eyes darted to the oxygen regulator . . . I set it up to twenty. Line valve showed flow . . . the bag was filling rhythmically with the sustenance of life.

Then I had to make a serious decision. Was the vision of Bud Briggs wriggling into Joan's undies really funny or was I feeling the first signs of oxygen trouble! Make up your mind! Make sure of your decision. All systems go, at twenty thousand feet I made my decision: yes, Bud, wriggling, squirming, and trying to hide, all at one time as I walked into the camper was a legitimate funny.

I sat back and enjoyed the rest of the climb to 24,100 feet. I was so elated. Not only had I made my gold altitude, but my diamond as well.

I got on the radio to announce it to the world. "Herb, it's Old Dog. I am starting down. I still have a little lift, but I'm coming down with a diamond."

I waited for his answer. Then I called, "Herb, if you read me click your microphone."

There was no reply.

The descent was as thrilling as the climb. Instead of going down through the window I decided to run on the wind. I turned the ship east and headed for the state of Maine. The sky east of the wave cloud system was all open, not a blemish in the blue. I stuck the nose down and cruised at an easy 100 mph. In twenty minutes or so I could see the Atlantic Ocean; Portland was down to my right. I made a 180° turn and flew back to New Hampshire. At Fryburg, Maine, I went under the wave clouds and put out the dive brakes to make my approach into North Conway Airport. I was never so tickled in my life. I'd been on top of the world, and was still there when I got on the ground.

I rushed to the phone when I landed and called Olive. "I made my diamond altitude," I shouted. She said some nice things about that and then I said a stupid thing. "Honey, I'm so happy, I'm going to buy you a diamond, too." Thinking about it that night I figured if she brought the subject up when I got home I could claim hypoxia.

We waited around the field until almost dark for Herb. He was having radio problems, so we figured he was forced to land out and couldn't let us know. Ted Pfeiffer was across the field getting someone's rig ready to hook the trailer on behind his car. We'd had word that at least two pilots were down, one over in Maine. As I went over to see if I could help, Steve DuPont asked if I'd like to celebrate my flight by joining him for dinner.

"What about Herb?"

"The phone will be manned until he calls. We can leave the number where we'll be."

Dinner started out with a few rounds of drinks and the usual gay talk that pilots have after a successful day. By eight o'clock I noticed that the table was getting quiet. I left to call the airport. There was no word about Herb.

After dinner we went back to the airport. Allan MacNicol had alerted the state police that we had a pilot down and if they got any word to call. We all sat around trying not to alarm each other. I told those who didn't know Herb as well as I did that if he was forced down in backcountry, he was very capable of taking care of himself. Not only did we all have survival gear along, but Herb was an accomplished mountain climber, an all-around sportsman, and in better condition than guys half his age. But by eleven o'clock I knew there was trouble ahead.

It was very late when Steve DuPont said to me, "Look, if he had a rough landing, deep back in some of this country, he'd stay in his ship and sleep there. He's dressed warm enough and with his food and water he'd know he could make it through the night. He'll walk out in the morning. That's what I'd do. Wouldn't you?"

I agreed because I wanted to, but then Steve ruined his own story by saying, "If there's no call through the night I'll meet you here at seven A.M. and I'll rent a small plane and we'll have a look."

It was a restless night. In those wee hours I awoke on several occasions. I knew exactly where Herb was.

The next morning Steve and I searched the west ridge of Mount Kearsarge—under the spot where I had dived out of the clouds the day before. We found nothing. At noon when we returned and there was no word, we knew we had a serious problem.

The Civil Air Patrol was called in and so was the New Hampshire ground rescue team. Gordie Lamb was flying in the area in his plane and heard the CAP was looking for volunteer search pilots. He flew in. I told him as much as I knew, and when an informal search was started in the afternoon, I went with Gordie. I wanted another look at Kearsarge.

By the following morning hundreds of people were on hand to help. The CAP organized the formal search. They briefed all the pilots on exact procedures and explained to spotters how to use their eyes. The FAA people interviewed me to find out as much as they could about Herb. The slowest plane with the most experienced spotter was given the Mount Kearsarge quadrant to search. At noon the search teams were called back by radio. I was again with Steve DuPont in a quadrant over Maine. When we landed back at the field we were only told that the mountain climbing team had been sent into the Mount Kearsarge area.

This ground team worked on a special radio frequency with the CAP. None of us was allowed near the radio room, but we could tell by the urgency and the faces as they moved in and out of the building that there was trouble.

Neil and Tommy Smith reminded the CAP that if the ground team found the ship they should not touch the instrument panel or the barograph. That was the giveaway to all of us that the ship had been found, because the officer they told it to ran to the radio room. Soon the commander of the CAP asked for a closed meeting. He wanted some soaring pilots in good health to volunteer to go in to recover the instruments. The damaged plane was found— but not the pilot.

I volunteered to go in with all my camera gear and photograph for the FAA. I was sorry I did.

Tommy Smith and Neil had to carry my cameras most of the way. It was a rough four-hour climb. Tommy, an engineer by profession, rigged up a sling to get me to the top of the tree where Herb's sailplane was lodged. I shot pictures of every inch of it. The damage was minor. Then Tommy was hoisted up and he gingerly removed the instruments. The barograph tracing showed the exact altitude that Herb left the ship.

The big question that night, and for many more nights, was: Why did Herb jump and try to parachute down from such a low altitude? He didn't have a chance. What went wrong? We'll never know the answers. We found his body days later.

I didn't fly for some weeks after that. I was having a drink with Gordie and he mentioned the fact that he hadn't seen me around the field. I told him the whole diamond affair had put me off.

"Look, Dick. You're really new at flying. I've spent my life at it. I took my training in the navy during the war. We were wiping guys out right and left. Sure, it bothered me and I had to do some hard thinking about it because I didn't want to be one of the numbers. The answer to it is this simple. The guys who got in trouble were not good pilots. They panicked when they got into a jam or they weren't paying attention to what they were doing. In this game you have to think your way right down to the ground. If Herb had stayed with his ship, he would have ended up with only a few bruises."

From all that I'd seen, Gordie was right. As we left the bar he said, "Let's go for the diamond goal flight, ninety-four miles out and ninety-four return. We'll run the ridge down to Pennsylvania and back."

I knew and Gordie knew that if I didn't get "back up on the horse and ride again" I wouldn't be much good as a pilot. We planned to meet at the field at 7 A.M. on Saturday.

I spent the next three days psyching myself to think *up*. I was even walking around on my tiptoes. This might have been good for my posture, but what it would do for me on Saturday was anybody's guess.

The morning was grand. A front had moved through on Friday night and we couldn't have asked for a better forecast. Gordie and I were in the air at 9 A.M. Three other guys went up at the same time. They left from Cape Kennedy for the moon. If they could make some 190,000 miles, I surely should be able to do 186 miles. By 10 A.M. they'd gone some 5000 miles and I was crossing the Delaware Water Gap into Pennsylvania—50 miles. Although Gordie and I were going to fly this together, I'd long since lost him. In Pennsylvania I ran into a head wind and started to lose some of that "up" confidence. One minute I was at 5000 feet feeling as though I couldn't do anything wrong, and a few minutes later I was at 500 feet grinding around in a weak thermal and praying. I was making more mileage up and down than I was cross-country. At the rate I was going, the sun would be down before I'd get to the out point, let alone the return. When I checked with Gordie he said, "Fly faster, you're bucking a head wind."

I got renewed confidence when I finally saw the Lehighton Airport ahead. I knew this country. That was the place where I'd landed and used Gleb's name. I got the best thermal of the day off that airport and it took me into Snyder's Farm—my turn-point—and then the ball game changed. I now had a tail wind the likes of which I'd never flown. Of course I'd had trouble bucking it! Now it was on my tail, shoving me home. Three thermals took me all the way back to New York, but I never allowed myself to think I was going to make it. When I crossed over the Delaware River at the Gap, both George Moffatt and Gleb Derujinsky were in the air to meet me. One got on either side of me. Gleb radioed, "Come on, we'll take you home." Two thermals later I was back into my local airport traffic.

My calculator had told me ten miles back that I'd made it. I refused to believe. When my crew called up to me and asked if I was going to finish the task, I answered that I wasn't sure yet. I was making that transmission when I was letting down for my landing pattern. I'd spent so much energy thinking *up* that I couldn't believe that I was now to

think *down.* I couldn't believe the impossible had come true
—186 miles.

One step for mankind, one for Old Dog.

I certainly made no speed record on that flight, but I did
break through my fifty-mile jinx—one-hundred-and-
eighty-six miles! Oh, how good that sounded at dinner that
night with all the flying gang at the spaghetti joint in town.
Now I had my gold badge, and because I made the distance
by preannouncing the turn-point destination, I earned another diamond as well. The three guys going to the moon
couldn't have had a greater sense of satisfaction than mine.
I wondered if Neil Armstrong, also a soaring pilot, was
wearing his gold badge on his space suit. If I'd been along
with him, I'd have worn mine. I had two diamonds on mine.
I started to believe that maybe I was a better pilot than he
was. Boy-oh-boy . . . two diamonds.

After I managed to settle down from my excitement,
taste my food, and get back to earthly thoughts, Gordie
asked me what I had done differently to get over my fifty-
mile slump. I thought about that for a minute, and then I
answered him seriously, "I think I learned something today. You know how we sit there in that cockpit, strapped
into a chute and then strapped into the plane—shoulder
and gut straps? I think I've been getting body weary. You
know what I mean?" I asked. "Well, today I sat there doing
exercises while strapped in. I learned to grind my back
around and flex my pelvis to relieve the tension. Gordie, if
I can translate what I learned in the cockpit today, into the
bed, I'll be a sensation!"

NINE

Some Weird and Eerie Flying

FRANK TAYLOR WAS AS THRILLED AS I WAS WHEN I TOLD HIM I could now send in my application for the national competition. Sixty pilots would be accepted and actually I might have a chance. There was one factor in my favor. The Nationals were going to be held in Elmira, New York. It would be very expensive for some of the pilots to come all the way from the West Coast to enter, so I might get a berth.

I was spending as much time in the air as I could. My problem was that I still wasn't consistent, especially in moderate weather. If it was a good day, like the gold badge flight, I could make it. I had to learn to fly in marginal conditions. That meant getting into the air on any kind of a day. This became very expensive. I knew that the ten days of flying the Nationals would cost $1,000 and there were some other regionals that I wanted to enter to get points. The key to my being accepted was going to be a decent score in a regional event—just one would do it.

I started to watch my pennies. I decided that six- or seven-dollar tows were getting expensive when you are talking about hundreds of them in a year. To go up and find that the conditions are so bad that it's a straight twenty-minute glide back to the ground wasn't going to help in any way. That was a waste. How does one learn to distinguish between marginal weather and useless conditions? You can't depend on the weatherman. That's no science; after all, meteorology is only to the meteorologist what astrology is to the astronomer. Predicting isn't easy, but I found a way.

I learned it from Ted Pfeiffer, one of the grand old names in soaring. It's this simple. He waits on the ground and lets the other guys spend their $6.50 for a tow. He notes the time of the early takeoffs and if they're not back in half an hour he knows the day is good. If the gung-ho types who take off early have radios, he'll call and ask how they are doing. Now, I'm not saying that Teddy doesn't have a real concern for their success or failure, but he also has a slight interest in saving $6.50. Take a look at his logbook: all three-hour flights. It's a foolproof system of "predicting" macrometeorology. But even his system boomeranged one time, and then the boomerang boomeranged on me.

It all started one day when the sky looked as though a $6.50 tow would be a pure waste of money. The field was deserted and working on one's ship in the hangar made more sense—so that's what four of us pilots were doing.

Someone just happened to notice that Teddy had rolled his sailplane out to the far end of the runway and was waiting for a pigeon to come along and test the air for him. The towplane was ready to go—but not Ted.

A quarter of a mile away, we four in the hangar decided to play a little joke on Ted. We switched on a radio in one of the planes, and started a conversation as we stood around the cockpit, inside the hangar, handing the microphone back and forth between us and using our competition call letters as though we were in the air. The conversation went like this:

"Leaky Water, this is Five Yank. What's your position?"

The microphone was handed to 5Y. "Leaky Water, Five Yank is behind you about two hundred yards and above. Flying with Old Dog."

Microphone handed over to GL. "This is some crazy air over here. Swing over to your right and get under me. Eight hundred feet a minute up . . . going through seven thousand feet."

Someone was posted at the door to watch Teddy. The microphone was handed to Old Dog. "Gulf Lima, are you in wave?"

"Old Dog, this beats me. It's not smooth enough for wave . . . too strong for cloud sucking, and I don't see how a thermal could be this strong with the overcast. I'm pulling out before I get into cloud."

"Five Yank . . . I got it! Four hundred feet . . . four fifty feet up. Got it, Leaky Water?"

"Affirmative."

"I can't find it!"

"Move over to your right, Old Dog."

A pause, then: "Got it."

With the microphone off, we all started to laugh so hard we couldn't talk anymore.

Finally Gordie said, "We're going to be a bunch of fools if Teddy doesn't have his radio on."

"He does," said the spotter at the door. "He's scratching his head and looking at the sky."

Finally Teddy opened his mike and called, "Hey, this is Blue Bird. Where are you guys?" You could hear the excitement in his voice.

In the hangar, Five Yank took the microphone. He closed his eyes in order to compose himself, then signaled for silence so our game wouldn't be discovered. He opened the mike and said, "Someone is coming through all garbled. Who's calling?" That broke us up all over again.

"Blue Bird . . . Blue Bird. Where are you guys?" came loud and clear.

Old Dog took a turn at the mike. "If that's you, Blue Bird, click your mike twice."

Click-click came the reply. Mac was holding his sides.

"Are you in the air, Blue Bird? If not, come on in—the water's sensational up at Ellenville."

Then the fun began. We watched as Ted raced to find the tow pilot and someone to run his wing. In a matter of minutes Blue Bird was airborne. Someone said, "Six bucks and fifty cents down the drain."

When he dropped off tow at three thousand feet, he called, "This is Blue Bird. I'm headed up to meet you guys." All of a sudden we knew we had carried the game too far.

"No," said Mac, "let him go. He can make the Ellenville airport, and we'll get his trailer and go after him." Then Teddy called again.

"This is Blue Bird. It beats me! On a day like this, I'm climbing through forty-five hundred over the fire tower. How long have you guys been up?" We stood at the hangar door, wide-eyed, mouths hanging open in disbelief, as Teddy in Blue Bird climbed out of sight in the overcast.

"Blue Bird to Leaky Water, I'm heading up toward Ellenville from five thousand feet. It looks strange up there. Can't see you fellows yet. I'm flying just under the cloud layer and getting zero sink. Fabulous conditions. It didn't look like this from the ground."

That did it—the four of us scrambled for our planes. We frantically swung wings on, made the hookup, preflighted, and rolled the ships into place down at the end of the runway. All the time we kept talking on our radios, keeping up the running chatter with Blue Bird, who was giving out all kinds of good information.

"Old Dog, this is Blue Bird. What's your position? I can't seem to find you. Have located a weak wave in front of a lenticular cloud. Very weak . . . smooth as silk . . . going up at two hundred feet a minute. Going through six thousand through the window in the clouds."

The four of us were towed off the ground in the fastest sequence of launches the field had ever seen. In the air, Blue Bird was singing the way. We all headed for Ellenville.

As we left the field, Gulf Lima called, "Old Dog, do you have any lift over there?"

"Negative."

"Five Yank, anything?"

"Negative. Heavy sink," answered Trux.

Blue Bird came back on the radio. "Still can't see you fellows. The wave action suddenly stopped. I got to seven thousand but I'd better get down through the opening before it socks over."

"Five Yank to Leaky Water. I'm heading back to the field. Nothing . . . absolutely dead."

"Will follow you back, Five Yank."

"Blue Bird to Five Yank. Looks like the show is over. I'm down below the overcast and find only heavy sink. Heading home. What are you guys finding?"

"It's all over, Blue Bird. We're all heading home," answered Five Yank.

And so five sailplanes landed back at the field one by one. That evening, over drinks, four pilots lied and tried to invent an explanation of the fabulous conditions of a day when no soaring pilot in his right mind would spend the $6.50 for a tow. We hung onto every word of explanation that Teddy gave, looking for a clue to the success of his hour-and-a-quarter flight. Blue Bird just kept repeating, "I can't understand why the sky went dead so fast at the end of the flight."

That lesson cost me $6.50, but I don't know what I learned. If it was marginal weather conditions I wanted to learn, I soon had my chance at the regional contest at Frederick, Maryland. The haze was so thick that you could cut it with a knife; the sun didn't have a chance to get down and heat the ground so that thermals were as hard to find as good-looking farmers' daughters. About the third day my score wasn't too bad because nobody was able to get very far. Then I made a secret plan. I took off and ran for the town dump. When I got there I could see the Frederick sanitation workers lighting the fire. As the smoke drifted up, I could see where the heat was. I got into the smoke! God only knows what they were burning that day, but it was making some stink and I sat right in it. The smoke filled my canopy and the stench filled my lungs.

Before I was about to get sick I saw that my secret was the same secret of about ten other guys. This day was going to be won by the pilot with the strongest stomach. I climbed inch by inch up that smoke wall and then had an idea; I really used my head. I put on my oxygen mask and laughed all the way up to the top of that mess. One by one, I saw the guys below were getting sick; they peeled off and radioed to their crews to go out on course. I stayed in the slop, climbing slowly, oh so slowly.

About the time my eyes turned into Bloody Marys, I peeled off and went toward Westminster. Already the radio was crackling with guys saying they were going down. I wasn't too high, but high enough that I couldn't see a thing through that haze. I navigated by compass on a 65° heading. When I glided down to about 2500 feet, the ground below was visible. I saw a sailplane down in a pasture. I thought to myself that at least that was one guy I was going to beat. I now navigated by the road below, but it wasn't necessary. A few miles ahead another plane was down. When I reached it I saw another and another ahead. They were pointing my way for me. Everything was going fine, except the stench was still in my cockpit.

Then something strange happened.

At nineteen hundred feet I felt a bump. I circled but couldn't find a thermal, so I went on. Still I was floating in

air that was going up. Another downed sailplane showed
me the way. I was back up to twenty-two hundred feet when
the lift stopped. On I glided. I put my chart away . . . I didn't
need it. More planes were below. As I passed over one
plane the pilot radioed up.

"Old Dog. Is that you?" I recognized UP, Art Hurst the
"chicken" pilot.

"Old Dog," I answered.

"How are you staying up?" he asked with wonderment.

"UP." I used his call letters. "When you smell me you'll
understand. I'm thinking of reversing *your* call letters and
using them."

It took him a few seconds to figure that out, then he said,
"Good show. Keep going!"

I clicked the mike to signal thanks. By this time I'd glided
down to nineteen hundred feet—and then it happened
again: I hit a bump and circled to find nothing. On I went,
but again climbing slowly as I went. This had to be some
kind of band of lift that no one ever told me about.

When I got over Gulf Lima on the ground, he shouted
up to me, "Go on, Old Dog. Go on!"

I clicked my mike and passed over him. Then I started to
think that possibly I'd passed over everybody. Oh no, two
more were ahead of me on the ground. I passed over them
with ease at twenty-two hundred feet. When I was on my
way back down to nineteen hundred feet, I thought I saw
Westminster through the haze.

"Old Dog. This is Old Dog ground," came Charley Coy's
voice. "Baby, we've counted twenty-five ships on the
ground. You've won the day. Keep going; chop their points
to nothing!"

I, of course, didn't want to seem a smug winner so I
didn't answer him: I just clicked the mike button. Even the
smell in the cockpit had turned to perfume—I'd won a
thousand points. The Nationals were a shoo-in for me.

As my plane hit the lift and I was on my way back to

twenty-two hundred feet, whatever it was stopped. It would now be a glide as far as I could go.

"Old Dog ground," I called after adding about eight more miles to my distance, "I'm low and going in soon. I have a field picked out. Do you read?"

"Go, Old Dog."

"OK, I don't know the name of the town that I'm coming to. It's on the road ahead of you. When you enter the town you'll see a big church. It has a gold cross on the spire. I'll land in the field in front of the church. In front of the church. Do you read?"

"We've read that, champ," Charley answered.

I might have smiled at Charley's transmission, but I'd cut things a little tight for the landing. I patterned on the left side of the church and on final whistled over the cross with about ten feet to spare. All was in good order; then I saw the field had much more of a dip in it than I'd anticipated. It rolled, but I'd have no problem because I had enough speed to hold the plane off the ground and pass over the hills. To my surprise, directly in front of me was a farmer on his tractor driving up out of the dip. He was going in the same direction as I was. I pulled back on the stick and used my excess speed to go over his head and land in front of him.

It was not actually a close call, but I knew I'd scared the daylights out of him because a sailplane's noise, the whistle, can only be heard behind it. There is no warning noise of an approach. I climbed out. I knew I could never get this farmer talking about his crops.

I started to walk back toward him. There he stood on the top of the knoll, hands on hips. At my distance I could tell his eye had the look of a wild bull and he was about the size of one. What a contrast he made with the church behind him. I remembered *The Hunchback of Notre Dame;* I felt like Quasimodo and smelled like him too; if I could reach a priest I could get sanctuary. And that's what happened.

As I was walking toward the farmer, who was glaring at me, waiting for my approach, I saw the priest in his robes come out of the church and walk toward us in the field. I slowed my steps so we'd get there about the same time, but before I reached the farmer he opened with a salvo, "God damn it. What in the name of Christ do you think you're doing!" he bellowed.

I didn't answer. I let the priest do the talking.

"Farmer Flannigan. Watch your language!" said the priest from behind.

Mr. Flannigan spun around. His hat was in his hand before he stopped.

"Father. Did you see this?"

"I saw *it* and I heard *you,*" came the soft reply.

"Why, I was so scared when that white bird flew over me head I thought it was Gabriel. I was so scared, Father . . . I was so scared *I prayed!*"

"It's about time, Farmer Flannigan . . . about time."

At that moment Olive and Charley rolled up with the trailer and some cold beer. Even Farmer Flannigan joined in on the toast to the champion of the moment, Old Dog.

I say champion of the moment because when I got back to the field, having already calculated my one thousand points, I was to discover that it had been declared a "no contest day." Regulations state that a day will count only if four pilots make a minimum distance of sixty miles. I was the only one to do it, so it didn't count.

I never did understand what kept me up on that flight. I told the story to the weather experts, experienced pilots, and to my rabbi. They all seemed to say the same thing, that there were some things we never get to understand. Bob Buck started to give me an explanation one night. It was sounding awfully complicated, and in the middle of it he stopped and said, "I don't know, there are some weird things that happen in the air."

Weird, strange, I'm not sure—maybe it's even something

more. I next went to a contest in the Blue Ridge Mountains of Virginia, seeking that score that was going to get me into the Nationals. Then this weird flight happened.

The countryside there was just as beautiful as Gren Seibels said it was when we talked about it at Sugarbush. Lanier Frantz and the fine people of western Virginia welcomed us in true southern style and made me feel like a Top Dog.

That first evening they told me much about the history and the traditions of New Castle—about iron mines that made it rich and the sheer beauty that made it a wealthy recreation area before the terrible war. Many of the old houses still stand. One could almost envision, from my hosts' descriptions, hoopskirts flitting about instead of hot pants. I liked the carriage and traditions of men like Lanier and Gren; our world, north and south, needs more like them.

In some ways they are living in the past. These men are very much in today's world yet there is something about their manner that seems to mix up time. The thing I liked about my short visit to their country is that they welcome you as part of it. After a few days you, too, feel their grand way and almost sense their tradition. Sitting on the lawn under their blanket of stars, listening to their stories told in soft voices, can carry you back to the grand time. With eyes closed you could enter a twilight zone. It was delightful but strange.

My first flight in that contest was strange, maybe even fourth dimensional, whatever that is. It started normally for me and ended that way, too. I went only nine miles but . . . I went only nine miles but it might have been backward.

After takeoff I climbed up to cloud base in a matter of minutes. Things were normal and started off like most of my flights. I gave my crew the secret coded instructions. "Hook up and go" meant hook up and go. The secret was, since I added no more information to their instructions, that meant I was lost . . . a little . . . and not sure which way I was going to go.

I then had a magnificent glide. I calmly screamed some last-minute orders to the crew as I sank below a ridge. "I'm going down in a bowl. Find a place on your chart where there are mountains in every direction." And so it was that I made my faultless landing under some telephone wires that were strung between trees—no poles.

I sat in the field collecting myself and waiting for a farmer's daughter to come greet me. After what I considered the proper length of time, I decided the farmer's son, wife, or the old crag himself would do. What kind of southern hospitality is this, I started to wonder? I took my pipe, chart, landing card, and a pencil and started to the house. I was right about instructions to the crew—there were mountains on all sides; they had a tall, quiet, peaceful look.

I had my best southern accent all prepared when I got up to the front gate, only to discover the house padlocked. "Goodness," I thought, "my thirty-fifth off-field landing and no farmer to brag to!" I peered in the windows; they hadn't been cleaned in years. The house looked as though it had been lived in that morning, yet the path to the front door hadn't been walked on in twenty-five years. Strange.

Up the road—well, I hate to call it a road, but that's what it amounted to—I spotted a sign. Walking to it, a quarter of a mile or so, I read that the town was called "End of State Maintenance."

I went back to the ship to get my road map. There was no such place listed. I made a mental note to write the Esso people a nasty letter when I got back to New York. I added to that another mental note: "If I get back." That house was too silent, unreal, furniture in place, plates on the table.

Since I could raise no one on the radio, I decided to set off. I had one brilliant idea. The telephone wires that could have caused me a landing problem would now help to lead me out. Off I went. They crossed a fence, so did I. They went through a wood patch, so did I. They crossed a stream, so did I. When they turned into a lane and led to a house, I smiled—but not for long. The house was full of furniture, deserted.

Back to the phone wires, but they ended abruptly, downed by a storm in the past. I continued across fields . . . across fences . . . streams, woods, up a road and over a hill . . . a path that more or less led to another house, empty! I knew, or thought I knew, there had to be a way—someone was still tending the land. When I got to a field with one cow in it, I thought I had it made. Someone had to milk her, or was she a bull? I decided to sit down and rest and take stock. I had my wallet and in the same pocket a candy bar. I had a chart and road map, but that's like having a dictionary and not knowing how to spell. I could tell by the moss on the side of the trees which way was north—or is it south? There was enough water in my left sneaker so that if the worst came I could at least get a drink. I also had a New York City transit token.

If she was a bull in that next pasture I wasn't going to find out. As I skirted the field, I spied a thin line of smoke back in the trees. On investigating, there was a house that brought to mind something Gleb Derujinsky told me many years ago: "When you have to make an off-field landing, select a house that has a TV on the roof. They'll have a phone." This place didn't have a phone, it didn't have paint: it was a one-room house of logs, boards, and tin. A thin old woman, in her rocker, with her old dog at her feet, greeted me from the porch. They may have seen better days, but the house never had.

There was no use trying to explain to her how I got there or what I needed. As we talked, she sat and rocked. I don't remember much of what was said because a strangeness persisted about the emptiness of this magnificent mountain bowl. I had the feeling it was as if it all were from another . . . She offered me water from a pail; it was the sweetest

I'd ever had. "Nothing like this in New York," I quipped, half-laughing. Her eyes left mine for a moment and glanced over the valley—her valley—left to her by her menfolk. I could have sworn her lips formed the word "north," but I never heard it.

Her bright eyes sparkled again; she gave me a toothless smile as she seemed to remember something. She reached into her apron pocket; its style and flowered pattern hadn't changed in generations. She offered me a cookie.

It would have been interesting to talk more to her, to find out who she was, how she lived, and for how long, but I remembered my crew and knew I had to get on with my business.

Opening my map I asked her to show me where I was. She was pleased and laid it across her lap. A few short jerking rocks of her chair conveyed her enthusiasm. With outstretched hand she rubbed her palm across the map and said, "Pretty! Real pretty."

I can't explain my reaction to her simple words. I brushed my thoughts away and asked her where I could find a telephone in the valley.

She looked up and cocked her head as if she didn't hear. "Telegraph?" she asked questioningly. "Mean telegraph?" she continued. "Hasn't worked since . . ." her voice trailed off as she was trying to recall.

"Phone," I interrupted, but then my wheels started to spin. It struck me; I'd been following what I thought were telephone wires, yet there were no poles. Telegraph, strung from tree to tree . . . Civil War . . . iron country . . . a rich country . . . a mountain bowl . . . a haven from disaster? Now empty.

She was talking, I was thinking. Then I heard her. "Ye better go up the road a piece to the Noel place. Noel sisters, them's rich. Went to school. Them should be able to help."

Somehow, I was on the road again. The mountains, as mountains go, weren't high, but they kept the world out—

rolling, rolling, as if there were no end; quiet, quiet like a secret; smoky color, like a protective lid. What story could they tell of the old woman or the valley?

Two miles later, the water in my left shoe was mud. I approached the Noel home.

The Noel sisters lived in a house that was gone with the wind. If the hedge were trimmed, if the mortar between the bricks were freshly pointed, if the forsythia were in bloom, if I had been walking down that road a century ago—or was I?—if they were wearing the same dresses, if there had been laughter, they would have been doing the same thing: playing croquet on the lawn that overlooked their valley.

I watched for a spell from behind an oak. I felt the part of an intruder—not to their game, nor even to their grandiose view of the bowl. It was something more—something out of my experience.

On spotting me, they stopped playing and stood erect, clutching their mallets to their breasts, but not out of fear. I had the distinct feeling that they had been interrupted at their game before, time ago. Even from my distance I could clearly see their dress was from another era, their faces as old as the house and as stately.

As I started up the lawn I stopped, because I had not been given the sign to approach. How long did I stand there? How statuesque they appeared—self-sufficient and strong. Did my long hair put them off? No. That's the way their menfolk looked during their war. Was I just another Yankee once again disturbing their peace, disturbing their mountains? Was I really flying only two hours ago? Am I real or are they real?

We never spoke, and for that I am truly sorry.

At that moment I heard a car on the road. It seemed so out of place, its noise so rude. But then I remembered. I called to the women, "Excuse me, ma'am," and ran to intercept the car and return to a time and place I knew.

The driver turned out to be an Army Corps engineer. On

the way to town he told me about how they were going to flood the whole valley and build a big dam.

"Another army is going to ruin the Noel sisters?"

"What?" said the engineer, giving me a look.

When my crew arrived, we had to carry the plane out of the field. As I drove out of the bowl, I tried to find both homes to show them to my crew. I swear I covered every inch of that valley. Finally, I agreed that the mountain woman's house would be difficult to see, but I became progressively angry when I couldn't find the Noel home or an area that looked as though it were near.

My crew chief, and chief wife, jokingly suggested that I *really* tell them where I had been for three hours.

Even now I have an eerie feeling about the flight. I only made forty points for the day. Did my sailplane play tricks with me? Did it take me nine miles in one direction—and a hundred years in another?

TEN

A Letter to Frank

DEAR FRANK:

Here is the letter I promised you about the Nationals. Better that I should have been with you in Paris. I might as well tell you right off that Old Dog isn't the new U.S. champion. If they awarded points for fantastic experiences, I might have ended up in the first ten; as it was, I barely made thirty.

As I told you, I entered the competition for experience with some stipulations: score be damned . . . play it safe . . . no damage to my lovely lady . . . learn . . . have fun! With all but one exception, as you will see, I followed my plan.

The opening festivities were very colorful and you would have been proud of me in my white flying costume. It was quite a spectacle to see fifty white fiber glass sailplanes lined up on the runway for the first takeoff. We were launched at one-minute intervals like clockwork. By the tenth day it was no longer a spectacle, it was a grind. Flying a National is harder than trying to make a living. I was up

each day at 6 A.M. and it was late to bed, absolutely exhausted. As for the weather, it didn't help. For ten days the
sky in this region looked like a milk pail with a mess of white
moths flying around in it.

I almost can't give you a full day-by-day report because
as I look back on it, all the flights seem to blend together.
As you know, Charley Coy couldn't make it as my crew to
work with Olive. Stupidly, he decided to get married. I still
feel if I'd flown better in those early contests he wouldn't
have gotten himself all worked up by changing the subject
and talking about girls every time I got scared of going
cross-country. I feel very responsible about sending him to
his fate. Meg Lippincott, the wife of Jim, who didn't have
a ship for this contest, took Charley's place with Olive.
There were many reasons why I picked her. Every once in
a while she helps Jim in his contracting business. She can
drive a semitrailer truck loaded with bricks and stuff around
the countryside faster and with more skill than any of Jim's
union drivers. She can repair a radio, swing a hundred-
pound wing as if it were a toy. I discovered she knew
enough, when I got upset about a day's task, to change the
subject and talk about men. Jim's a great guy, but after my
experience with Charley I hope her talk won't break up
their marriage. Oh yes, I had one other reason for picking
Meg . . . I was the only pilot in the contest who could kiss
both of his crew members each morning. It didn't make me
many points, but I sure enjoyed the sport.

I can't remember where they sent us on that first day's
task. It really doesn't matter; I never got there anyway. I'm
not even sure how I finally made out on points. Oh, I could
look it up on the score sheet, but that's not what I mean.
I won't really know how I made out until my wife either
decides to forget the matter and/or to confront me with it
directly. I'm not even going to tell you where I landed that
day . . . and you'll see why.

There I was, flying high and sassy over Binghamton with

over sixty miles checked off my chart and the "milk" got so thick that I had to dive to stay out of the clouds. Well, that must have done it for me. I started to get into trouble in the air, but nothing like the kind of trouble I was going to get into on the ground. There is no use going into all the details of the flight, but I did change direction and radio that information to the crew. Then I lost contact with them. When I changed course I headed north because I thought the conditions looked better up there. They weren't. At that time, I remember thinking, as I changed course again to get back on my original flight plan, "I hope the gals won't cross the border into Canada." Boy, am I sorry they didn't.

At a town, I was trapped in nothing but heavy sink. I gave it the old college try and ran for the ridge on the outside of the nameless town—no lift. Then, flying over the center of that hamlet, I looked for heat rising from the few bunched buildings—nothing.

Below were at least ten good farms from which to choose. The one I picked had been hayed the day before. The wagon marks were still clearly visible. I made an eight-hundred-foot pass over the chosen field. It was fine: good approach, no wires, no posts, gullies, or rocks. The wind was light. The gear was dropped and locked, dive brakes tested, and the circuit was started. The touchdown was sweet and gentle—no last-minute surprises.

Before I had the canopy off, a good-looking farmer's boy was already there, wide-eyed, mouth agape. I broke his spell by calling, "Is the farmer home?" I was half tempted to ask if his sister was home, too. With my luck in all the contests, I've still to land in a farmer's field where his daughter was older than eleven.

The ship was secured to the fence near the gate. I glanced at my watch: 5:30. There was no time to lose. Goodness only knew where my wife and Meg were. My first business was to call the field and give them my exact location. When the girls called in they'd find out where I was and come get me.

The farm boy helped locate my exact position on the sectional chart. He witnessed my landing card, one of two signatures needed, and then I asked him about a phone. He didn't have one at home, so he directed me to a pub down the road a piece.

With map and landing card in hand, I trotted off. Time was now the important commodity. About one mile from a coronary, a local farmer in his pickup stopped and gave me a lift. When I told him where I was going—the bar up the road—I could see him draw back as if from the devil himself. That was the end of our conversation. When we got there, I could see why he was so appalled. If I were driving on this road, dying of thirst, I'd pass this dump up.

I wasted a few minutes getting my eyes accustomed to the gloom of the place. Spotting a phone by the door, I made my call. When I hung up, I looked at my watch and wondered how long it would take the crew to find me.

Frank, you know how long I've had to wait for my retrieve on some occasions. Sometimes it was hours. One night Gleb slept in his ship in a contest out West, and you know, as good-looking as he is, that had to be a pretty dull place.

As I turned from the phone, my eyes acclimated to the dim interior, I did a double take. Was it a mirage? Had my flight caused hypoxia? Was I dreaming? Did I have an accident on landing? Was I dead? Was this heaven, or could it be hell?

The room was empty except for one figure—and some figure it was—behind the bar. I was stunned. There stood the most resplendent woman I had ever seen, even when I was alive. Her body seemed to erupt from the gloom. And I stood there with my mouth looking like a parachute bag, afraid to talk for fear of slobbering.

She smiled, she spoke; her voice was as rich and as round as the rest of her. "Looks as though you need a drink."

Possibly my eyes rolled, as I was now completely convinced that I had crashed. Groping slowly toward the bar, I was conscious of soft rock music in the background. Rock music in heaven? Impossible—but, except for my crew chief, with my luck with women in life, that's where I'd have to be in death. A woman like this in heaven? Again, impossible. Then it all came to me, but it was a shock. It's the devil himself—he's a she!

In one last desperate effort, I gathered all the facts at my command.The landing had to be good: good approach . . . wheeled her on . . . short roll-out. Of course I was alive! No one could be dead with this woman. I glanced at my watch for reassurance that I was in this world; ten minutes had passed since I came in.

All was well—all was really well. I whistled under my breath that old song "Time on My Hands," then smiled at my new acquaintance, and reached for the cool beer she had drawn for me.

We talked. She was fascinated just by the thought of my flying in a motorless plane. She made it seem so important. Then we swapped names. Leonore—like a Beethoven overture. The name Old Dog caused a burst of laughter. She tossed her head back, her hair swung rhythmically, her eyes sparkled with the fun of the name. Oh, how I prayed for a five-hour wait.

I told her about soaring contests. She leaned on her elbows, cradling her face in her hands, and was so attentive. It became difficult explaining how a contest works. I forgot all about telling her how a crew works. Then I remembered my landing card and asked her to be a witness. She was so pleased. Like a child, with pen in hand, she looked up at the ceiling for a moment to get inspiration and then she wrote: "To Old Dog: I attest that Old Dog landed here on July 6th at 5:30. A gift from heaven. Love, Leonore."

Then, Frank, she did a wonderful thing. Under her signature she wrote, 36–22–36. Since I was using my competition numbers, she was using hers, too.

She handed me the card. I read it, smiled and looked up at her—but our eyes didn't meet. I followed her gaze past me.

There stood my crew chief. Next to her stood the first mate, Meg. All of her rigid 150 pounds was scowling. I got a look that would knock a tail off a sailplane. Then she folded her arms across her bosom and gazed around scornfully with her mouth open.

Smiling to all, my crew chief came forward and thanked my hostess for taking such good care of her pilot. They shook hands. The darts flew. Then Meg announced proudly that she believed it was the fastest retrieve, without a radio, on record. Just my luck.

Okay, you've got to give them credit, they figured out with some good guessing what I'd do. They guessed right. If I'd gotten my wish, a five-hour retrieve, would they have guessed what I might have tried? And Frank, that's why I refused to name the town. Someday I may just go back and catch up on the clock before some other soaring pilot does.

I'm sure I didn't win many points for the day; in fact, I may have lost some. My crew didn't talk to me except by radio for two days. The second day's task was a speed triangle from Harris Hill to Cortland, Tri-Cities, and back to Harris Hill. That's when I started into one of those jinx patterns. I landed at a place called Newark Valley, an area I became very fond of. In fact, I dropped in on those charming country folks so often in the next few days that they had my picture taken for their newspaper, called me by my first name on the second trip, and offered me a contract to bring in their mail on the third.

It was just like South Royalton, Vermont. Every time my plane went near the place it started to go down. By the third day or so of these shenanigans, I decided it called for a change in my strategy. I started yelling at my crew. It didn't do any good. They almost mutinied, and I almost ended up washing down my own ship. After a hard day's work I only got to Newark Valley; that third day was declared a no-contest day because fifteen pilots couldn't manage to stay in the air long enough to make the required sixty-mile flight. This was the first day I could brag how well I did because we all got the same points, zero. I was now starting to relax about the contest since I had made rather good off-field landings. I started checking them off . . . seven to go and no damage.

Of course in the contest we were not allowed to help each other by radio, but there were other ways. The "help" the lovable competitor from Pennsylvania with the incredible name, Ice Berg, gave me I could do without. In fact, he owes me a thermal in our next contest. Here is the way that came about. Bud Briggs, Roy McMaster, and I were minding our own business together at tree level just past Corning. Gleb came in under us, so low that he must have been singing "Tiptoe through the Tulips" to himself. I soon joined him on the chorus. He found some lift and we were both saved. We flew on together and, just to be sociable, I found lift and he joined me. I wish Ice played the game that way. I stayed with that thermal, but Gleb left and went on. I knew he made a mistake because I worked it up another thousand feet. Even the big boys can make mistakes. As it turned out, my score for that day was 235 points; his was 912, so you can see how bad his judgment was.

While sitting on top of the world fat and arrogant, who should fly by but Ice. In the next eight miles we flew together and found nothing. At Campbell we worked the town, a factory, an open pit, road construction, some beer joints, and couldn't even find zero sink. I finally turned to my radio and said, "Ice, I've got a good field and am going to dump." He answered, "I'll follow you in." I banked my loving bird over, slid between two trees holding the left wing up until the tree was passed, leveled off, and touched

down. I mentally checked one more landing off my list
. . . six to go.

Over the radio Ice said, "Beautiful landing, Old Dog.
You held that wing up over that tree like a real dog. I'm
right behind . . ."

That was the end of his transmission. I took off my
canopy and looked back to watch his landing. He wasn't in
sight. Looking up I spotted him.

"Thanks, Old Dog," Ice Berg blurted over my radio.
"You kicked off a thermal when you landed. Thanks, see
ye."

When I returned to Harris Hill that night the bad news
reached me before the car stopped. Art Hurst had cracked
up his ship. The good news was that he wasn't hurt. We
waited and finally at 10 P.M. he arrived with his wounded
bird. It had taken two hours to carry the ship off a ridge.

God, Frank, that scared me just when I was getting over
the fear of the off-field landing. Art was in fourteenth place
when it happened. He is one of the best competition pilots
in the country. That's when Meg started to talk about men.

The next day, Joe Conn, our contest director, affection-
ately called Uncle Joe, named the task for the day: Speed
to Dansville and return.

Moffatt was still leading the pack. Every day one of the
local wine companies presented a bottle of champagne to
the winning pilot. I'm not even sure what winery it was. The
way I was flying I didn't have a chance, so I never gave it
a second thought. Except, I did think that if air is a fluid,
a few corks might help me stay up. George won eight bot-
tles of champagne. Now I know what they mean by "get
high and stay high" to win contests.

To my surprise, I too got champagne. I got to Bath and
was shot down. It's the same old story, no need repeating
the details except for the landing. I was circling over a
power station in Bath. I radioed my crew, who were parked
under me waiting for me to disappear down the stack, to

drive up the road and find a landing spot. I had a schoolyard in range, but didn't like its looks. Then someone
turned off the power station and the stack gave a final belch.
I radioed down to step on it, and then said forget it. I'd go
myself. I glided north into a fine field. A farmhand gave me
a rough time and I knew from his description of the farmer
that I was going to have an encounter again. I did. Ted
Spore, the farmer, came out into the field in his Cadillac.
He got so excited by this happening that he presented me
with a bottle (chilled to 56°) of Widmer Gold Label champagne, and took the next day off and crewed for me with
the girls.

I checked off one more . . . five landings to go. But I had
food for thought. Another pilot landed in that schoolyard
in Bath that day and a second ship was now out of the
contest! Demolished.

By the next day the routine of the contest was established; it consisted of work, work, work. The outside world
was shut out. Contest director Uncle Joe Conn was General
Staff, Justice Department, and legislator all wrapped into
one little ball of energy. His biggest problem was with his
department of weather. One forecast could have sufficed
for the whole contest: a stagnant high-pressure system sat
over the whole of central New York. Thunderstorms were
predicted for the afternoons and/or visibility diminishing
in smoke and haze. We were supposed to fly only VFR
(Visual Flight Rules). For us VFR meant Vision Fully Re-
stricted.

That day there were forty-five white moths in the same
bucket of milk, never to touch each other. One at a time
each would fly to the surface and off to Tri-Cities, the first
turn-point. That's what the gaggle-and-start gate was like
over Harris Hill. Navigating to Tri-Cities is usually a simple
matter. There is a big river to follow if needed, but you
couldn't even see it this day. What seemed to be good
clouds took me a little north off course. I was some lost. I

radioed to my crew every thirty minutes, saying, "Old Dog
ground." Including the word "ground" in my transmission
was my signal to them that I was still in the air but only God
knew where, and I was hoping He cared. Flying by compass
and my watch, I then headed south. In ten minutes I was
directly over my turn-point—sheer luck. At first I was
stunned, then I decided it was skill. I could tell from the
radio that many pilots were lost. I was elated with my good
fortune. Now I'd show Moffatt and the big boys how to fly
this course. I told my crew to head north and to step on it.
I headed up toward Newark Valley, a course I could fly
blindfolded. And . . . I must have! Shortly my crew had to
find a field for me. I was in real trouble. I'd thought I knew
this valley, but I had no place near to set the plane down.
I called down to them—they were driving on the road right
under me. "Old Dog ground. I got trouble! Can't see any
fields ahead." That's when Meg's driving ability paid off.
They never answered my call. I was flying at fifty-three
mph. In seconds they were doing ninety-five. I had only a
few minutes more and I was going to be in the trees.

"Old Dog, this is Meg. Now listen carefully. I have a field.
It's small but you can make it. You will not see it coming
from your direction. I have you in view now. Follow the
road. Keep coming. When you come to tall trees that form
a lane start a slow turn to your right. Yes, your right."

I was flying up the valley, not very high over the
housetops. Then I saw the trees she was talking about
coming up. I saw the trailer and the car parked in the
middle of the road. Meg was on the roof of the car with
radio in hand.

"That's good, Old Dog. There is no ground wind. Keep
your flight slow. Hold that turn until you get over the house
with the red roof. Look to your left now! There is your field.
You have telephone wires after the trees. Then drop her in.
Good luck, baby!"

It was a postage stamp field. Frank, that is as close as I

ever want to get to that situation again. If these national contests were only for spot landings, I'd have won the champagne that day. I took pause that night when I checked off four more landings to go. Was I getting cocky?

The task next day was speed: Tri-Cities, Sidney, and return. For me the day proved to be another milk run, in more ways than one. I got lost again in the murk and I flew my usual course to Newark Valley. Oh, God, not again! I swore then that on the next flight if, when I asked the farmer on landing where I was and he answered Newark Valley, I'd bash him in the teeth.

When I got low, I didn't even have to take out my chart to see where I was. I recognized every fence post. Well, there's nothing like being "at home with friends," but I should have known that sooner or later my long hair was going to get me into trouble with these country people.

Here's how that took place. As I came in low, I tried the town for lift . . . nothing. I tried the ridge . . . nothing. A plowed field . . . a sawmill . . . nothing! I wanted to go home and hide. Wasn't I a Gold Badge pilot—even with diamonds? Sure I liked the folks in Newark Valley, even their daughters. I'd still like to meet some other people—further east.

As I flew over my old neighborhood, I remembered something Bernie Carris said the day before. When you're low, look for a pond. The differential of air temperature over the pond and surrounding land will often kick off a thermal.

There it was below me; why hadn't I seen it before! A perfect setup: a pond with fifty kids swimming, a hayed field, road construction, and even a ridge. I went for it. Now I'd show them!

I got over the pond. How cool those kids looked. I started to fan out. I knew just as sure as the sweat was pouring down my face that my vario would start to sing an up tune. I tried the road construction . . . no song. I tried the field . . . no music. I tried the ridge . . . not even an off-key Yankee Doodle. Beethoven, where are you?

I decided to try again. I worked over the pond. I worked over its edge. I worked it downwind. I worked it upwind. I worked that pond so low that I could see from my vantage point which were the big girls.

So, with no musical accompaniment, I dumped into the hayed field. I consoled myself. Good landing. Right up to the road. At least my crew couldn't complain. Three more landings to go.

I was very hot, my hair was matted down on my cheeks. I just sat there in the cockpit with my hat and canopy off to catch the breeze. It was then that I saw the kids swarming out of the pond and racing for me. I just waited for the onslaught. What else could I do? One boy, the biggest, led the pack. I thought that if I could fly as fast as he could run I wouldn't be in this predicament. Down the road they came, all shapes and sizes. When the speedy one got within fifty feet, he stopped dead in his tracks. He turned to the frantic procession behind him, cupped his hand around his mouth, and shouted to them, "HEY, WAIT TILL YOU SEE THIS. IT'S A LADY DRIVING THE MACHINE. SHE DON'T HAVE A MOTOR, BUT SHE'S GOT A MOUS-TACHE!"

It wasn't the kids making fun of my long hair that had me down in the dumps. I didn't let on to the other pilots, but down deep I knew I could fly better. Being satisfied with good, and at times even spectacular, off-field landings wasn't enough. Gleb kept saying to me, "Think *up.*" I was doing that so hard that I was getting light-headed.

We got back to Harris Hill that night in time to swim. As I walked toward the diving board I told my crew to stand by. I told them I was about to try my second sport for the day and with my luck I might need a retrieve.

Frank, I was getting tired and I knew that was when I had to be careful. I had a restless night's sleep. I kept doing a speed task all night. I went around the course four times, zooming across the finish line with tremendous speed. Harris Hill went crazy with excitement. Uncle Joe came up in a towplane and awarded me two thousand points. I went around again. What no one on the ground knew was that I couldn't get down. I was soon frantic. I did everything: skidded, slipped, dove—all up. But the dream ended okay. I converted the Harris Hill setting to Newark Valley and down I went, *fast.*

The seventh contest day was going to be my day; I could feel it in my bones as I threw my back out putting the ship together. It would be the first day to see Moffatt fall from first place. Ed Seymour, the airline pilot from Rochester, would fly 131.7 miles in the prescribed area and Bernie Carris would do 121.5. George would be behind Bernie by only 1.5 miles.

I took off late. I had luck, I could see ten miles ahead. I flew fast for this weather, seventy mph. I joined a gaggle at Horseheads. Left it fast. Joined a gaggle at Cayuga. Climbed and left it fast. Next thing I knew I was calling in over Ithaca. At Dryden I got on Gleb's tail, things got scratchy, but we survived. I found a thermal and he joined me. Gleb found one, and so we went. On to Cortland, he found a beauty but I couldn't seem to core it. Up he went and off he went. I started to stumble around. I finally made a save. Another plane joined me. It was George Moffatt. The weather northeast of Cortland started to look bad. I heard Briggs call his ground and say he was at Truxton. That was on my course, so I decided that I'd try it into the overcast. George did the same. I got on his tail. Somewhere between Truxton and De Ruyter, George suddenly changed course and flew north. I figured he didn't want me on his tail and was trying to shake me. I held my course for Hamilton, my first turn-point. I couldn't give any other explanation for George's change in course. Then I saw some ships working a thermal. He had gone to join them.

But a bad storm was coming in from the north and it looked like curtains. I stuck with my decision, hit the best thermal of the day, and went to cloud base.

That was the last I saw of any other sailplanes. I was back in the milk and navigated by compass and clock. All I could see was the ground below, and it had a sameness to it that made the chart useless. Briggs radioed that he was going down at De Ruyter. I thought the storm must be hitting. I veered southeast to stay out of its way. All I could say to my crew was to stay on course. They must have known by the way I was passing cities that I had gotten out of my Newark Valley slump. My first landmark through the crud below was a college. I figured I had navigated wrong and was over the town of Eaton. I pointed the ship east to get away from a violent thunderhead and consulted the chart. There, to my surprise, was the word "college." I was dead on the town of Hamilton. I couldn't see the town, the two lakes, or the airport. They were engulfed in black. I made a fast decision. Fly in, get the turn picture. Get out, and ride in front of the storm. I could feel my heart start to pound as I shoved the stick forward. I charged my white Libelle against the black wall. I went down under the gray froth and there was the town, the two lakes, my airport. Rain splattered on the canopy. The streets in town were still dry. Maybe I could make it. Lightning struck north of town. Two miles in and two miles out. At 120 mph. One minute in—would the rain hold off for 60 seconds? It was so black I wondered if the Instamatic would record the picture. Who cared? I had other problems. One second the canopy was drenched and I was blinded, the next instant it was clear. Another gush like that and I made up my mind to turn and flee.

One mile to the airport, it looked dry. It was a head-on race between me and the storm. I pushed the nose down . . . I could feel the winds slam into me. It was as black as night. "Stay alert," I was saying out loud. I was blinded for a second by a flash of light and the instant cannonade had my heart going as fast as my ship. "Keep going! Go." We were having a contest, that storm and I, and I was winning. I took my turn picture from a weird angle and leveled the wings for the flight out to the light. What a thrill! But I made an error. I didn't know how to fly a fast-moving storm. I got out too far in front. If I could only have ridden that storm south. I searched for lift out in the brighter sky. I turned back toward the storm, but it was too late; I was too low. The blackness caught up with me. Now it would be a race to get the ship tied down. I landed on the top of a ridge in an isolated field, deliberately flying parallel to the line of posts, and touched her down two feet from the fence. I jumped out, grabbed a rope that I carry, and tied the baby to the fence. I didn't bother to mentally check off one more safe landing . . . two more to go. This landing proved to me that I knew my business about off-field landings.

When the storm hit me on the ground it blew so hard, rained from all directions, it filled my mouth with water, couldn't speak. Farmer Mish was soon by my side. We were both drenched. He came up the ridge on his tractor. Mrs. Mish had the hot coffee perking by the time I arrived. After the storm passed, John Daniell put his plane in the same field and joined us for coffee. "You weren't crazy enough to go in for that turn picture," he said, in his charming English accent. I just drank my coffee and smiled, knowing I had beaten George to the turn and that Gleb had gone down near Bud Briggs. I was eighteenth that day.

Frank, let me interrupt to tell you that since I'm home from the contest I wondered how safe I was to dive under that storm. I really wouldn't have questioned it, except when Farmer Mish called the local paper to tell them what he had on his farm the editor rushed out. Over coffee the editor really did battle with me and told me I was a fool to have done what I did. "I flew in the war!" he kept saying.

I tried to explain that I was never in danger. I had the speed and altitude to get out at any second. He ended the interview with the statement that it was unsafe. I answered that I was safer than he, driving his car out to the farm on the wet streets.

I just received a letter from Farmer Mish. When the editor left to go back to write his story, he was almost killed in a car accident. It took hours to get him out of the car and at that writing the farmer only knew that both the editor's legs were broken. I only tell you this since you were so concerned about the safety of this sport and wanted me to make sure I covered that in my book for you. Frank, more miles were flown in contest than there are miles around the world. Five ships were cracked up in the contest, but no one was hurt. No one!

So, with that I will tell you about the last day. I was so pleased with my ship; I knew she was still better than I was. I'd forgotten all about keeping score on just-one-more-safe-landing to go. If I could handle the gaggles in the murk we were flying, and the landings I had had, the last day could bring no surprise.

The weather was going to cooperate—possibly—that last day. I scurried to get charts ready to take me all the way to Vermont. I told my crew, "Dinner tonight with old friend Jim Herman at the Sugarbush Inn." I was itching to get off. The sky looked as though it was popping northeast. Once in the air, I told my crew to get moving. I headed out over Horseheads. Conditions weren't as good locally as they looked, so I decided to play it safe and let the weather develop. A wisp formed off to my left. I headed north and went to cloud base. Someone was already being shot down below me.

The day just never developed. It looked good but it wasn't. Fifty miles out I was getting into trouble. I'd flown over this same country with Bob Tresslar a few days earlier. We had gotten in trouble then, run for a ridge, and worked a thermal back up. I headed for the same spot. It was dead. I was low . . . this was going to be my big day. I moved to another hilly section and caught some zero sink. Saved! I spotted a hawk, the best thermal spotters in the world, and went to work. He went up a hundred feet and I went up with him. What a piece of good luck. Below, I had a choice of three fields, but I wasn't going to need them. The hawk ticked off another hundred feet, so did my beautiful baby. The hawk dropped a few feet, flapped his wings, and moved over. He had company: I moved with him. He seemed to be having a little problem. The fields below were a comfort. I made my choice. The one that had been mowed the day before was the longest. The fresh grass cuttings were still lying on that field; it had to be good. It had a slight uphill grade, no wires, no rocks that I could see. It had a uniform color, so it had no ditch. Satisfied that that would be it if needed, I went back to work. My hawk was holding his own; so was I. I figured I'd sit it out and wait for the thermal to make up its mind. A great decision—my only choice. Down deep I felt confident. Hadn't George talked about doing this at the pilot meeting? If need be, I could stay with this one right down to pattern height. The wind was drifting me slowly into a good pattern situation for the selected field. We two hawks, a redtail and a white beauty, held on to-gether for ten more minutes. Then he gave up and flapped off. "Quitter, quitter!" I half said. I shook my fist at him, wishing I could flap off too. I stayed on my own, but my vario started telling me the truth.

Well, Frank, that was the contest. I'd have to go in for the last landing. I could not bring out the best my great white bird could do, but we learned a lot together. It was a fantas-tic ten days, an exciting colorful experience—score be damned. Sure, one takes a chance. What are you going to do, stay in bed—alone? I was sorry the contest was coming to an end.

I dropped the gear, cracked the dive brakes, and held

them in. I went through my landing procedure, which included reading the sign I have over the gear handle: "Wheels down? Stupid!" From here on down it was duck soup. Landing number nine! The last!

On final I opened the dive brakes. Airspeed sixty . . . OK for a no-wind day. Ten feet over the trees . . . over the trees . . . full brakes. Field looks good . . . slight upgrade, remember flair . . .

The instant before touchdown, I think I remember seeing that the grass was high. It had been mowed the day before with a combine machine, not a mower as any city boy could tell . . . from the ground. I touched, rolled, and ground-looped. Nothing very hard, only 90°. I sat there a moment and listened to Gleb talking to his crew. I called him. "Gleb, will you tell Old Dog's crew that I'm down."

I got out and was surprised at the height of the grass. I decided to get down and check the gear doors. I came up with a smile on my face. All was well. Then I saw it: the tail of my beautiful lady was broken in half. Frank, I cried . . . I think.

My best,
Old Dog

ELEVEN

The End of Old Dog

A MONTH AND A THOUSAND DOLLARS LATER MY BEAUTIFUL
lady and I were together again. I hadn't let *her* down on that
landing and she had done right by *me,* too. What had happened was I was a better pilot at flying than the farmer at
his farming—a rock in his field broke her.

Flying the National was very important as far as writing
my book was concerned. I had learned a great deal in all
that marginal weather. I kept practicing and working hard
all through the following winter with my eye on the Sugarbush contest in the spring.

The finishing touches were being put on the training
book, and Frank and I were spending a lot of time together.
One evening I said to him, "I hate to see this project come
to an end." Of course, I was remembering what it was like
between books. "I have a funny feeling about it."

He looked up from the manuscript and asked, "What do
you mean?"

"Well, I don't know. I *really* don't know." And I really
didn't. It couldn't be the flying. Actually, all the pieces were

coming together. I could go up and stay up in almost any kind of weather. The fear of landing out never bothered me now. I'd lost track of the number of times I'd set my Libelle down in all kinds of places, and I was finding it was the furthest thing from my mind. I wasn't even doing off-field landings anymore now that I was completing all my practice tasks and getting back to the airport.

The book, *The Art and Technique of Soaring*, was finished when the snow was too deep to fly, so I went to Sugarbush. On Washington's Birthday I took a ski tow to the summit of the mountain. Resting at the gondola house at the top of this world, my eyes drank in the vast expanse—hundreds of square miles of rugged, lonely, silent terrain, dormant in its winter dress. How well I knew this place. I took a deep breath and steeled my nerve for the long slide down into the valley.

Memorial Day, three months later, the height of spring. I was towed again to the top of this sea of trees: but this time, instead of in a fiber glass gondola on a cable, it was in my fiber glass ship on a two-hundred-foot towline behind an L–19. It was the last day of the contest and at the start a situation developed that didn't help matters.

My selected takeoff time was 12:02, and at that time I set my panel clock as my crew lifted the wing, signaling that all was ready. I wagged my rudder as confirmation to the tow pilot to move out. As I waited, eyes glued to the towplane, Charley, who was back crewing for me, lowered my wing to the ground—a signal to hold operations.

I thought, "What the hell is he doing? Ships have to be launched at two-minute intervals. If a pilot misses his time, he then has to go last; that's the rule of the contest." Then I realized that something was happening. People looked frightened, they were pointing. I glanced at my wife, who was on tiptoe trying to see. Looking anxious, she ran over and took off my canopy to keep me from being cooked alive.

"Someone is coming in for a landing, and he's awfully low," she said.

"Some trouble," said Charley.

Finally I could see the problem from my low position in the cockpit. A competitor with an earlier takeoff time was coming in for a landing and relight. That is normally a routine and unremarkable event; but one look at this situation and I knew there was trouble coming. What in the name of heaven was the pilot doing? Why hadn't he landed downwind on a day like this? Or cut his pattern short? "Take your options!" seemed to scream through my mind —but no, someplace up in his head this pilot was hearing his instructor say, "Make a full landing pattern." With the plane at treetop level, his long downwind leg forced him into a base and final legs that were no more than a 180° turn. Sucking in my breath, I measured the distance of his lower wing tip and the ground that came up to meet it with a crash . . . a sickening noise.

My canopy was snapped shut, roll time reset for 12:03, eyes glued again on the towplane ahead. As we moved down the runway, I took a split second to glance over: the pilot was climbing out of his smashed bird. "At least he's OK," I thought, "but what a way for me to start a flight over this kind of country!" Then I wiped my mind clear and went to work, retracting gear, switching on instruments.

The tow told me much about the day. Over the open valley the climb-out was as steady as an elevator. As soon as we hit high ground, the towplane took a leap up. Three seconds later, at the other end of the towrope, I was in the same updraft. My vario pegged; it was going to be a strong day. This told me that the valleys would be dead, and the action would be over the high land.

At 2000 feet I dropped off tow and raced back to the spot I had marked as we towed through a thermal. It had enough lift to take me to 5000, fast—but there were better ones around. A mile or so across the ridge five planes were climbing even faster. I flew over and joined them, bottom man in the heap. I punched the stopwatch and recorded the altimeter reading: 550 feet per minute of actual climb—the strongest day ever of my Vermont contest flying!

I was ready to go through the start gate. The task for this day was a speed triangle from Sugarbush to Rutland, then Jay Peak (a ski resort near the Canadian border), and back to Sugarbush, some two hundred miles.

"Sugarbush Gate, this is Old Dog one mile out."

"Old Dog, you making a left turn?"

"Negative. Straight in."

"Got you spotted, Old Dog."

At 120 mph I wasn't losing altitude fast enough to get under the top of the imaginary start gate at 3100 feet above the ground. I shoved the stick forward to red line and hoped for a little sink to help get me through.

"Good start, Old Dog!" came from timekeeper Bob Rose on the ground.

The zoom up was a thrill. I headed for high ground. I knew the first leg to Rutland by heart. This flight follows the mountains south over very rough terrain. Looking down I could see there were absolutely no landing spots. It was over the spot where I almost learned that fiber glass birds don't nest too well in trees that a good thermal hit me in the seat of the pants. I banked over, ground around, and circled up in it to eight thousand feet.

Ten miles across the valley and down the ridge of mountains, I caught the flash of a sailplane wing circling at almost my altitude. He was my mark. I headed south at one hundred mph, straining my eyes to catch the flash of his wing in the sun. When I got there he was gone, and I'd lost three thousand feet. I ran for a bowl-shaped ridge with a north face, swept into the bowl, and made a long, slow turn above its rim. My audio variometer sang for joy, its panel needle danced! Pulling into a tight circle the thermal was cored . . . up . . . up . . . up. In ten minutes I was back at eight thousand feet, with the satisfaction of knowing that I'd figured out where the thermals were to be had. Having made forty-four miles in about as many minutes, the first leg was almost in the bag: from there it was a matter of getting on the west side of the mountains to the safety of the Champlain Valley. By hugging the high country, two more thermals would have me over Rutland Airport. I searched out every bowl-shaped mountain that faced north. My theory kept working.

At no point during the flight had I gotten low enough to figure out the lower limit of the strong lift band, but I could guess from my observations on tow that below four thousand feet it would take hard work to stay aloft. I soon found out!

Since the lift was over high ground, the valley was full of sink. Before rushing out for the turn-point picture over Rutland, I searched the terrain for another bowl-shaped ridge that faced north; I found one three miles past the airport, but its lift was weak. Figuring weak lift was better than none, I dashed for the turn-point, taking the picture as quickly as possible, then scurried back to my weak thermal in the bowl. My heart sank; it had recycled and was gone! Now, at only three thousand feet I knew I could reach safety, but to stay in the contest I had to find something fast! Should I go cautiously back toward the safety of the airport in the valley to look for lift, or take the chance of the higher country? This was the three and two pitch.

For the next fifteen minutes I sweated it out over the mountains with barely enough lift to sustain my altitude: the lift was there, but somehow the strong part of it eluded me. It was extremely frustrating!

Another plane flew in for the turn picture, then came out of the valley as if to join me. If he thought I had something, he was in trouble. Within a quarter of a mile of my position he banked into a 45° turn and started to climb. That was all the help I needed. I radioed to him, "Thanks!" And he responded with, "Come on in, the water's fine."

It was slow, but up we went. Then I got a strange radio message from him. "Old Dog, I'm going in at Rutland. I'm sick."

I hung around and watched him all the way to his touchdown and radioed to his crew that he was on the ground and safe. Now I had to climb out of the low country alone, over the range of mountains to get back into the high ski terrain. I practically clawed my way up the sheer wall that ran all the way to the Canadian border. It wasn't just a matter of clearing the peaks—I needed enough altitude to reach the safety of the farms deep in that country. I'd gain some, then lose—gain and lose. "God," I thought after a half hour of this yo-yoing up and down, "maybe I should get sick. Why put myself through all this?"

My back was starting to break. My white lady was fragile to pit against these mountains, but she had style. We worked on and then something nice happened. A thermal took us up to six thousand feet just about the time I was convincing myself that it was all over. Once through what I figured was the band of weak updrafts, I was back on my way, feeling a little sassy again. I radioed my crew to head north and they, too, knew what that meant—to the border. I caught up with three other ships and for two-thirds of the way north we had a delightful flight together. We stayed in the strong lift band between six thousand and eight thousand feet. When we got down to six thousand, we'd peel off in different directions, quartering the sky; and when one plane found lift, the others joined it. We couldn't do anything wrong.

By four o'clock the thermals were definitely getting weak. The radio came alive with frantic pilots giving landing instructions to their crews. I was now in country new to me; about fifteen miles from the Canadian border sat Jay Peak, my next turn-point. The chart showed no bowl-shaped ridges facing north, and I was headed into the wind. Putting the altitude and distance into my computer, it said I could make the turn-point, and that was about all. I went for broke.

This was the most frightening terrain I had ever encountered. Instead of flying from mountains out into a valley for the turn-point picture, it was necessary to fly west into higher mountains to get the picture. Ahead was nothing but forest, and I was getting low enough, or the mountains were coming up fast enough that I could see a woodsman cutting trees. Behind was farmland and safety (oh, how I wished for a rearview mirror!). I knew I could always make a 180° turn and fly out east, since the terrain fell off at the same rate as my plane's glide ratio. The situation looked much worse than it was because I was flying head-on into the trees—up a narrow valley to the ski slope. At only a few hundred feet over the parking lot at the bottom of the ski slope, I stood that ship on its wing tip for the picture, and got out fast.

My watch said 5:08. Too low for any high country searching. I zigzagged in and out of every ridge on the flight east to safety, then I turned south. This was the last leg—less than fifty miles to go, but it looked like the end of a magnificent day. The radio was coming alive again with pilots falling out of the sky, calling their crews. I radioed my crew for their position and sent them on to Lowell. If I didn't find something in a few minutes, I too would have to cut out into the flatlands and set her down. Oh, for just two more eight-thousand-foot thermals and a tail wind to get me home!

Then I inched my way toward the high country, but was forced back to the farm country. When my crew radioed their position, saying they had me spotted and asking for instructions, I told them to find me a field that looked good. I soon found them; they were parked beside the road and I was low enough to see my wife standing by the car, binoculars trained on me.

"Old Dog, we're parked by a good field. The wind is from the north at about five. Make your pattern and come over the trees to the south of the field . . . no wires, no posts. Drop it in fast . . . the far end of the field looks wet."

"Thanks. Coming in."

I dropped my gear and went through my landing plan. On downwind I hit a bump!

The "instructor" in the "back seat" was saying don't pay

attention to lift once you have started a pattern. The "pi-lot"—in command—made a fast decision: all was well, there was height enough for one 360° turn to try the lift. If the bump didn't turn into a working thermal, I'd drop her right into the field.

Altitude was sustained in the turn. Hurrah! I tried it again, switching off the radio so as not to be distracted.

Half of the second turn was in lift, the other half in sink. I shifted my circle by flying an ellipse, then tightening into a steep bank. Stick forward . . . can't afford slow speed at seven hundred feet . . . move to the right . . . around again . . . varios were showing zero sink in the poorest quadrant of the turn . . . things looking better . . . get ground refer-ences . . . that barn . . . move to the right . . . move with the drift of the wind . . . the thermal is being pushed by the wind . . . too far, too far! HOLY COW, pull up the gear! Move the ship to the left . . . eight hundred feet . . . hold it, stay in it . . . one hundred feet per minute of lift . . . slow up, tighten the circle . . . bank 'er over . . .

At four hundred I turned on the radio and called the crew, "Old Dog ground."

"Old Dog, ground. That was a great save!" Charley said.

Old Dog knew it and was pleased, but didn't have time to enjoy the feeling.

"OK, move south slowly. Need about five more of those to get home. I'm headed for high ground."

"Keep going," Charley answered. "My new wife won't let me talk about girls."

My watch said 6:12. I'd fought that spot for almost fifty minutes. The tail wind was helping now, but only an occa-sional last bubble would be going up at this hour. Flying the ship's best speed L/D, if I could only reach the north face of the Hungry Mountains . . . The air was dead. My mouth was dry. My calculations showed that I needed four more thermals like the last one to get me home. . . .

With thirty miles to go, I reached the Hungry Mountains by the skin of my teeth and found a dying thermal waiting for me. Ever so slowly, I climbed back to four thousand and gingerly went on. At Stowe (twenty-six miles to go), another bubble. Back up to four thousand and drifting toward Waterbury . . .

Into the computer I put altitude, 3800 ASL; distance to go, 23 miles . . . Sugarbush field elevation 1470 . . . with a straight-in landing I had only 2300 feet to do 23 miles? Impossible! I'd been flying six hours. I was going to lose it at the last minute.

Hanging over the high ground on the edge of the valley that was a direct run to Sugarbush, the variometers showed zero sink. The air was dead—but something was happening. I passed Waterbury with a loss of only a few hundred feet; at Duxbury I was down on the ridge with a wing tucked into the trees, but not losing much altitude. What was holding me up? My best glide ratio alone wouldn't do it. Then I figured it out. Cool evening air was replacing the heat of the valley, and the warm air was drifting up the ridge, holding me up! Absolute defeat was within seconds and success within inches. If it would only hold, I'd have it made!

It was no longer in my hands. There was nothing more I could do. Either I made it or would be forced down two miles short of the airport into Ed Eurich's field. For a fleeting moment I recalled that first off-field landing. Then I'd made two miles, now I'd made 206. Oh, how I wanted the last two.

I turned on the radio.

"Sugarbush Gate . . . are you guys still there?"

"Who's calling?"

"Old Dog, two miles out. What are your ground winds?"

After I'd announced that it was Old Dog about to finish this longest task in the contest's history, Bob Rose at the finish line opened his microphone to give me landing clearance instructions. Someone standing near him had heard my transmission and hollered, "OH, NO. IT CAN'T BE OLD DOG!"

"Old Dog, this is the tower," Bob answered me. "Winds light. Land to the north. Where are you, Old Dog? Are you really coming in? We can't see you! Where are you?"

"Low," I answered, pleased to hear all the excitement in his voice.

"Old Dog, I've got you spotted. God's sake, KEEP IT COMING!"

"Tower," I radioed. "Bob, clear the runway, baby. If I make it, it's going to be a straight-in landing."

I was so low I couldn't even see the field. I moved over closer to the ridge.

"OK, Old Dog, land straight in. KEEP HER COMING."

But I never did land straight in. One mile out something happened. Something was thinking *UP* as hard as I was, and the last of the valley heat swelled up the ridge and lifted me into full view of the one spot in the world I wanted most.

I opened my radio. "Old Dog, one mile out . . . making speed finish!"

"Beautiful, Old Dog, BEAUTIFUL" came Bob's excited voice. I never heard him talk so much on the radio.

I stuck the nose of my lovely lady bird down, aimed her for the finish line. She responded, liking my easy touch.

The speed was poured on . . . 120 mph . . . 130 . . . 140 . . . red line. She was aimed dead center over the runway. At twenty feet off the ground I leveled her off as we crossed the finish line. We zoomed by the tower. I couldn't take my eyes off our flight path.

The radio burst. "Great show, Old Dog!"

Carefully now, I gently pulled back on the stick. My grand lady lifted her nose and all I could see was sky . . . up . . . up . . . up . . . until all her speed was burned off. We traded 140 miles per hour for a thousand feet of altitude. She raised one wing as if in a salute to the nice things that were being said on her radio. A chandelle and a wing over brought her gracefully into her landing pattern.

"Gear down," came Bob's voice as the landing gear was dropped. I touched her onto the runway, rolled her, and she stopped on the apron.

Instantly I was so tired that I had to fight to get the canopy opened and off. Then I heard it! Every automobile and even the field siren were blowing and blasting. What a tribute to my lovely lady! I was so exhausted mentally and physically that I could have cried with joy. Tired and weary, I just sat there. I didn't have the strength to lift myself out. Never before had I heard them welcome a ship.

Charley ran up—more than that, he flew across the ground—"First place!" he shouted. "FIRST PLACE!" he whooped over the blasting of the horns.

That night at the party at the Sugarbush Inn, my friend and contest director Jim Herman and his contest manager, lovely Rachel, presented me with a decorated cake. My white lady, sculptured in fluffy sugar, was streaking over a green mountain. She was writing Old Dog in the sky, but she had changed her flight and crossed out the word Old and printed in a bold flight, TOP . . . TOP Dog.

Before my favorite crew chief and I went to sleep that night I muttered something about not liking it.

"What don't you like?"

"Top Dog. I think that's what I was trying to say to Frank Taylor."

"What are you talking about?" she asked.

"I liked Old Dog. I liked the people we met and the jams we got into. Winning is fine, but believe it or not I miss the fire department, Farmer Flannigan and his priest, Billy Penn, the kids who thought I was a lady, God, that terrible coffee in Plowsville, the farmer who thought I died, fighting with the press, and even Leonore—I was her five-minute gift from heaven, thanks to you.

"When you finally learn to soar you stay up and miss all the fun down here . . . Did I ever tell you about the wonderful farmer's daughter I met on that long wait I had in Maryland? When I landed and went up to the house and met the farmer, he let me use the phone and then went out to finish his chores. His lovely daughter was fascinated with my plane and the whole idea of my visit. She fetched me water, and knowing I was going to have a wait brought me some cookies. I took her out and showed her everything about my plane and then she asked if I'd like to see the farm. We walked out to the barn to see the cows. Her face was so expressive as she told me about the sheep. Her blond hair flowed in the breeze as we walked down the lane, hand in hand, toward the pond to see the horses. I knew she liked me and I liked her. She thought Old Dog was a funny name. What a lovely eight-year-old!''

Top Dog? I wonder if I can get Old Dog back?

Dear Frank:

Sorry I haven't written for these many, many months. Actually I misplaced your address. I hope your new publishing venture works out well for you. Did you hear how well our book has been doing? The first year's report shows that it did just as well as you said it would: it's going into its second printing! I'm not sure that we've got the public barking all over the sky as you had hoped, but soaring is becoming very popular—as we predicted.

Frank, I met a guy on my commuter train the other day who told me an exciting story. He'd spent the weekend in New Jersey learning to fly a hot-air balloon. It sounded great, so I went down and had a flight. It's a whole new world! What an exciting experience! We drifted at housetop level, talking to the people below. Then we floated over farms and woods. One family having breakfast on their patio called up and invited us for coffee. Down we went, and this time the coffee was good.

I've checked on it and there is no good book written on ballooning in this country and I was just wondering if . . .